Franklin Benjamin Hough

History of Duryée's Brigade

During the Campaign in Virginia under Gen. Pope, and in Maryland....

Franklin Benjamin Hough

History of Duryée's Brigade
During the Campaign in Virginia under Gen. Pope, and in Maryland....

ISBN/EAN: 9783337064211

Printed in Europe, USA, Canada, Australia, Japan

Cover: Foto ©ninafisch / pixelio.de

More available books at **www.hansebooks.com**

HISTORY

OF

DURYÉE'S BRIGADE,

DURING THE

CAMPAIGN IN VIRGINIA UNDER GEN. POPE,

AND IN

MARYLAND UNDER GEN. McCLELLAN,

IN THE

SUMMER AND AUTUMN OF 1862.

BY FRANKLIN B. HOUGH.

ALBANY:
J. MUNSELL, 78 STATE STREET.
1864.

EDITION THREE HUNDRED COPIES

PREFACE.

A participation in the exposures, hardships and perils, incident to army life, naturally tends to the formation of a fellow feeling, which time only strengthens and confirms. When these associations are broken up, the memory will still dwell with melancholy pleasure upon the scenes of privation and danger, through which we have passed, and although they may be succeeded by others of equal, or perhaps greater hardships, these early events will still remain deeply traced in the memory, as being the first experience in the soldier's life, and attended with circumstances full of novelty, and therefore more vivid in their impressions. After the pleasant associations formed under the command of Gen. Duryée had been broken up, many officers expressed a desire to preserve some souvenir of these relations, and the subject of adopting a badge, for designating those who had served in the Brigade, was at one time under consideration. The general orders establishing a peculiar badge, for each division and corps of the army of the Potomac, were issued while this subject was under discussion, and the adoption of this measure, rendered this course inexpedient.

In the summer of 1863, when alluding to the services of the Brigade which he had commanded, General Duryée expressed to the writer of this volume, a desire that he would undertake to place upon record, in permanent form, the leading facts connected with its organization and services.

The volume here offered, is the result of this suggestion. It has been much delayed, by causes depending on scarcity of labor and material, incidentally due to the existing war.

In typographical neatness and general finish, it is hoped that this little volume will meet the expectations which the conditions of the prospectus promised, and that in the general accuracy of its statements, it will accord with the recollection of those who participated in the scenes which it describes.

CONTENTS.

CHAPTER I.
Biographical Sketch of General Duryée,   9

CHAPTER II.
Organization of the Brigade — Expedition to Front Royal, .   29

CHAPTER III.
The Army of Virginia — Advance to Culpepper — Battle of Cedar Mountain, ... 39

CHAPTER IV.
Retreat from the Rapidan — Battles of the Rappahannock Station and Thoroughfare Gap, ... 69

CHAPTER V
Battle of Bull Run, August 30, 1862 — Retreat to the Defences of Washington, ... 94

CHAPTER VI.
Campaign in Maryland — Battles of South Mountain and Antietam, ... 106

CHAPTER VII.
Encampment on the Potomac — March into Virginia — Reorganization of the Brigade — Conclusion, . . . 122

CONTENTS.

APPENDIX.

Officers of Brigade Staff, and of the Several Regiments — History of the Formation of the Regiments — Casualties in Battle; Lists of Killed and Wounded — Official Reports, Col. McCoy, (previous to Augt 31) — Gen,Duryée (South Mouetain and Antietam) — Capt. MacThompson, (South Mountain) — Col. McCoy (to Adjutant General of Pennsylvania) — Biographical Notices, Dr. J. T. Heard, Col. C. Wheelock, Lt. Col. J. P. Spofford, Capt. R. Jones, Lt. L. Dallarmi, Col. H. Carroll, Col. T. A. Ziegle, Col. T. F. McCoy, Lt. Col. R. W McAllen, Capt. J. T. Dick — Second Battle of Bull Run — Battles of Maryland — Extract from a Letter, 131

ERRATA.

Page 42, middle line, for *Van Allen* read *McAllen*.
Page 42, 6th line from bottom, for *Northrup* read *Northup*.
Page 43, 5th line from top, for *T. M. Fuller* read *J. M. Fuller*.
Page 48, top line, for *Bufort* read *Buford*.
Page 184, 14th line from top, for *Gauto* read *Garita*.

DURYÉE'S BRIGADE.

BIOGRAPHICAL SKETCH OF GENERAL DURYÉE.

A preliminary sketch of the life of Gen. Duryée will doubtless prove acceptable to many who served under his command in Virginia and Maryland, through the arduous campaigns of 1862. The materials for this, have mostly appeared in newspaper articles and other printed form, but in none so fully as that which we now offer.

Gen. Abram Duryée, was born in the city of New York, April 29, 1815, and is descended from a family of French Huguenots, who emigrated to America upon the revocation of the edict of Nantes by Louis XIV, 1685. This cruel and arbitrary measure, deprived France of many of her best citizens, and these exiles on account of their religious faith, laid the foundation of several of the most prosperous settlements formed under the Colonial Government of New York. The Allaires, Bayards, Le Roys and Delanceys of New York, and the Hugers, Marions, and Legarés of South Carolina, trace their ancestry from the same source.

Young Duryée received a liberal education, at the High School in Crosby Street, and in the Grammar School of Columbia College. In 1838 he was married to Caroline E. Allen, daughter of William Allen, Esq., by whom he has four children, one son and three daughters. His son J. Eugene commanded the 2d Maryland Regiment in the Campaign under Burnside in North Carolina, in that under Pope in Virginia, and under McClellan in Maryland.

Gen Duryée commenced business as a mahogany merchant in New York, in which pursuit, by industry and perseverance, he has been eminently successful and is still engaged.

He commenced his military career as a private in the 142d regiment New York Militia, under Col. Graham, and was soon promoted to General Guide, Quarter Master Sergeant, and Sergeant Major. In 1838, he joined the National Guard, then 27th Regiment Artillery, as a private, and remained over two years in that station. He subsequently passed through all the grades of non-commissioned office, with approbation, and on the 21st of Feb., 1840, was made Second Lieutenant. Passing rapidly through the grades of First Lieutenant, Captain, Major and Lieutenant Colonel, he succeeded on the 29th of January, 1849, to the command of the famous Seventh Regiment. During his term as Lieutenant Colonel, he commanded a Battery of Artillery, consisting of six guns.

The Seventh has long been a favorite regiment in New York city, and during the eleven years that it was under the command of Col. Duryée it not only sustained, but greatly increased its wide and deserved reputation, for efficiency, discipline and moral bearing, in which, it has not been surpassed by any military body in the country In his management of its affairs, Col. Duryée evinced much industry, and great military and executive ability. The Regiment became, in fact, a military school for the volunteers of the army, and over eight hundred officers, from Second Lieutenants to Major Generals, who had belonged to the Seventh, have served in the army in the present war, from motives of undoubted patriotism, and with a success that reflects honor upon their earlier training in the duties of the Soldier.*

Col. Duryée commanded the Regiment in the memorable and bloody riots at Astor Place Opera House in 1849, where he was twice slightly wounded with stone. The effectual manner in which the riot was quelled by the decisive measures of the Seventh Regiment on this occasion, gave to it a prestige which has ever since been a terror to all disturbers of the public peace of the city In the Police and Dead Rabbit riots of July, 1857, at the City Hall and Sixth Ward, this Regiment was again in active and efficient service. In fact Gen. Duryée has been engaged in the suppression of every riot in the city of New York, for the last twenty one years. He was Commanding Officer at Camp Trumbull, New Haven, Camp Worth, Kingston, at Newport, Rhode Island, and on two excursions to Boston to attend the celebrations of Bunker Hill and Warren Monument celebrations.

* See Appendix.

In the summer of 1858, the Seventh Regiment formed the escort of honor, that accompanied the remains of President Monroe to Richmond, to which place they were removed from New York, under a resolution of the Legislature of Virginia. The circumstances attending this event derive additional interest from the contrast which three years wrought in the social and political relations of these cities, and will justify some extracts from the volume that commemorates the details of this transaction.*

The Regiment was welcomed on the deck of the Steamer Ericsson upon her arrival at Richmond, by Col. Mumford, in a heartfelt and touching speech, in which he said:

"The citizens of Richmond welcome you to the Capital of our Mother Virginia. The circumstances under which you have come among us, are calculated to make a deep impression, and to excite the kindest sympathies of our hearts. You are paying sad honor to one of our illustrious dead, and though his voice is still, and can give you no thanks, yet a mother's love receives you with open arms, and a nation greets you with gratulation and praise.

We have not been unmindful of the kindness and courtesy of our brethren of New York. When this, one of Virginia's sons, had served in every position of honor within her gift, ascending step by step to that eminence from which the virtuous and pure shine more conspicuous and brilliant, and the vi-

* An elegant volume of 324 pages, printed at the expense of Mr. Udolpho Wolfe, and embracing every document and fact of interest connected with this event, was presented to each member of the Regiment.

cious and selfish more glaring and odious, your state testified its favor, and twice voted to place him among the purified and illustrious. And when he, after having controlled millions of public treasure, retired to private life in poverty and want, seeking the rest which public service denies, your city received him in her bosom, and he found that repose which he coveted in one of your family circles, where filial affection ministered to his wants, and the kindest friendship soothed his declining years.

And when on a National Jubilee, in the midst of rejoicing for our National Independence, when gallant troops were marching to the enlivening strains of National Anthems, and our orators were animating and revivifying all with ennobling patriotic sentiment, and high hopes and aspirations were leading the gay multitude to enjoyment and mirth, then, when it was suddenly whispered that the good and illustrious statesman had just breathed his last, that jubilee was turned into mourning and grief. Those rejoicings were hushed and still, the gay battalions returned with colors shrouded to the tap of the muffled drum, busy men paused in their career, and none would be satisfied until highest honors were decreed to the dead, or until they were paid, with touching pathos, at the funeral and the grave. The remains were embalmed with a sister's tears and a sister's love. And now, after a lapse of years, when the mother comes to reclaim the bones of her dead, and asks that they may be permitted to repose in her bosom, until they shall rise in immortality, the sister with willing heart, decrees them a victor's triumph; her battalions vie with each other in demanding to be the guards of honor; another National Jubilee is shrouded, her orators again utter eulogies in his praise, her young men and maidens gather roses and laurels and strew them around the bier, and the incense of devoted hearts ascends to heaven. What an occasion for renewing fraternal friendship, for pledging the mutual fidelity and affections of Revolutionary times! How happy will it be, if the bones of our mighty dead shall prove a permanent cement to our Union!

And if at some future time, Virginia shall bring, as she hopes she will, to the same spot, the remains of her Jefferson and her Madison, and lay them side by side with those of Monroe, and the other Presidents who were born within her borders, shall be brought by kindred hearts to repose in her bosom, with her other great sons, and the people of every sister state shall make their pilgrimage to her shrine, to pay reverence and respect to her Washington, and their Washington, and to these her sons and their sons, then will the Union be knit indissolubly together, and the powers of the earth may wrestle with us in vain.

You gentlemen have commenced the great work; you are the guards of honor who attended the first of her sons to his home. We have the mournful pleasure of returning to you, as the representatives of your state, the cordial thanks which all have so justly merited and won. We give you the welcome of grateful hearts to our city and our homes, and beg you to carry back with you our kindest remembrances."

To this speech Colonel Duryée replied:

"In behalf of the Seventh Regiment, I thank you for this generous and cordial welcome. We are indeed honored in being permitted to escort, as a guard of honor, the remains of one of Virginia's most illustrious sons, one who obtained the most exalted rank that can be conferred by a free and independent people. In the person of the late President Monroe were combined the rare qualities of Soldier, Patriot, and Statesman, whose devotion to his country, and fidelity to this glorious confederacy, entitled him to enduring honors and imperishable fame. Indeed, well may Virginia welcome with honest pride, the remains of her noble son.

"Accept again sir, our sincere thanks for this kind reception, and the honor conferred upon us by the constituted authorities of the city of Richmond, which will ever be remembered as a public mark of respect by Virginia to her sister state."

After partaking of the generous hospitalities of the warm hearted Virginians, the regiment returned by way of Washington, where they were reviewed by President Buchanan, the Cabinet, the Foreign Ministers, Army and Navy Officers, and other dignitaries. Before leaving, they visited the tomb of Washington.

On the 4th of July, 1859, Col. Duryée offered his resignation, which was learned by the regiment with deep regret, and they waited upon him in a body with urgent solicitations for him to remain. Their efforts were unavailing, and his purpose was fixed.

In his retirement he became the recipient of compliments and testimonials such as no other officer has received. The merchants and bankers of New York presented him with an elegant Service of Silver, with the following testimonial:

"To COLONEL A. DURYÉE,
 Late of the Seventh Regiment National Guard:
 The undersigned, merchants and citizens of New York, feeling that you have conferred great advantages on the city, in the devotion which you have shown in the cause of citizen soldiery, in developing that *espirt de corps*, which now so happily exists in most of the regiments of the city, and particularly in bringing the Seventh Regiment National Guard, while under your command, to its present high state of discipline and efficiency, beg the acceptance of the accompanying pieces of plate, as a testimonial of their appreciation and esteem.
 New York, Dec. 24, 1859.

B. AYMAR,	GRINNELL, MINTURN & CO.,
D. JONES,	SPOFFORD & TILESTON,.
AUGUSTUS SCHELL, .	E. D. MORGAN & CO.,
ALSOP & CHAUNCEY,	HOWELL L. WILLIAMS,
A. T. STEWART & CO.,	MAITLAND, PHELPS & CO.,
DANIEL F TIEMAN,	JAMES G. KING & SONS,
J. J. ASTOR,	GOODHUE & CO.,
BROWN BROTHERS & CO.,	HERRICK & CO.,
L. DELMONICO,	BARCLAY & LIVINGSTON,
DUNCAN, SHERMAN & CO.,	CHAS A. HECKSCHER & CO.,
MOSES TAYLOR & CO.,	PELLS & CO.,
AUGUSTE BELMONT,	HOWLAND & ASPINWALL."

 Col. Duryée also received from his associates in arms, a testimonial of surpassing beauty, a masterpiece of workmanship in silver, consisting of eleven massive pieces, a dinner service, costing five thousand dollars. Accompanying it was the following address engrossed upon parchment:

"*Col. Duryée:*

Sir—After an uninterrupted service of twenty-one years in the Seventh Regiment, National Guard, you have recently closed, in the very vigor of manhood, a brilliant military career. Acknowledging your well earned title to repose, we yet deplore the necessity which has made your right to that repose superior to the claims which have so long held you in the military service.

Holding to the truth of those principles of government which admonish us of the necessity of a well regulated militia, and recognizing in your services those well and faithfully discharged duties of the individual citizen, which alone can give success and perpetuity to our national institutions, and feeling the obligations so eminently your due, and being desirous of expressing those obligations in a manner which will prove sincerity, the officers and members of your late command have deputed us to present you this testimonial as an evidence of the appreciation of your long and distinguished services, your untiring devotion to the arduous duties of your high position, and the military distinction you have conferred upon the regiment. Our earnest desire that the testimonial should be worthy of its recipient, has delayed its completion far beyond the time originally contemplated. It now only remains for us to perform the agreeable duty of delivering to you this evidence of our regard for your high personal character, and eminent military qualifications. Your three years connection with the regiment as a private resulted in your rapid and successive promotion through every grade of office, until yuo reached the highest in our gift; each promotion showing in turn, how well every duty had been performed, and how soon your soldierly qualities had been recognized. Eleven years of continually increasing usefulness at our head, and a withdrawal, accompanied by demonstrations of regret of an unprecedented character on the part of the regiment, and followed by a substantial token of regard from the most respected of our fellow citizens, constitute your title to the esteem of the Seventh Regiment, and of all who honor it. The many years it was our pleasure to serve under your command, form a period of prosperity in our history, which in the past was hardly to be hoped for, and in the future will be remembered with pride. But far dearer to you Sir, we know, than any testimonial however costly or elaborate, is still the welfare of our corps, and far more acceptable than language of compliment however sincere, will be our assurance that the lessons of duty and discipline inculcated by you, will never be forgotten; and that it is our purpose by renewed exertions to maintain unimpaired that high reputation, for the enjoyment of which we are so largely indebted to your exertions.

We deliver to you this tribute, as a pledge of our sincerity, and a token of our esteem. Receive with it also our best wishes and fervent hopes for your continued prosperity and happiness in every relation of life."

To which Colonel Duryée replied: —

"*Colonel Crawford and Gentlemen Committee.*

How inadequate is language to convey to you the sensibility of the heart, touched as it is by this expression of esteem. My old companions in arms, you who have toiled with me, you who have achieved honor, glory and renown, for your regiment, you who have so often made my soul thrill with pleasing emotions by the music of your step and the ringing of your arms; if ever the human heart possessed grateful emotions mine leaps forth its thanks in response to you now. This magnificent gift, so beautifully appropriate in its design and execution, reflecting great credit upon the gentlemen committee, the artisan and manufacturer, is indeed a memento that will pass from generation to generation, reflecting in its own glistening lusture the characteristic munificence of the National Guard. But, gentlemen, there is another testimonial accompanying this service of plate, of which I am exceedingly proud. The complimentary address is not so passive in its character; for it speaks. I shall prize it equal to any thing I possess. I accept with heartfelt thanks this beautiful testimonial from the Seventh Regiment. May your future be as brilliant as your magnanimity, and your actions continue as high toned and elevated as your surpassing generosity."

Col. Duryée remained in retirement until the breaking out of the great rebellion, when he at once resolved to enter the field. He began to organize, discipline and drill a volunteer regiment, enlisted for two years under the first call of the President, and known as the 5th Regiment, or Duryée's Zouaves. A recruiting office was opened in New York city April 23d, 1861; and on the 9th of May the entire regiment was mustered into the United States service by Capt. Seymour of Fort Sumter fame, and now a general. The reputation of Col. Duryée, as an accomplished officer, hastened the recruiting, and in sixteen days a full regiment was received under a rigid examination from over three thousand men who offered. After a month's instruction in garrison at Fort Schuyler, the regiment enbarked on the 27th of May, on the Steam Ship Alabama for Fortress Monroe. On arriving there, Col. Duryée was placed in command of the troops of Camp Hamilton, as acting Brigadier General. The command consisted of Col. Baker's California Regiment (71st Pennsylvania, Volunteers) and the 1st, 2d, 3d, 5th, 10th, and 20th, New York Volunteers, amounting to about six thousand men. They were thoroughly instructed in outpost and picket duty, battalion movements, and evolutions of the line.

Gen. Ebenezer M. Pierce having arrived, was ordered by Gen. Butler to assume command of the Brigade, and Col. Duryée returned to his Regiment: On the 9th of June, at 8 o'clock P. M. Gen. Butler summoned the Commanding Officers of Regiments to his Head Quarters within the fort, and there announced to them his purpose of marching on Little and Great Bethel. The following plan of attack, was the production of the unfortunate Major Winthrop, and was read to the Officers for their guidance; no specific orders having been issued.

"Notes of the Plan of Attack.

"A Regiment or Battalion to march from Newport News, and a Regiment or Battalion to march from Camp Hamilton: Duryées. Each Regiment to be supported by sufficient reserves under arms in camp, and with advanced guards out on the road of march.

"Duryée to push out two pickets at 10, P. M. one two and a half miles beyond Hampton on the county road, but not so far as to alarm the enemy; this is important. Second picket half as far as the first. Both pickets to keep far out of sight as possible. No one whatever to be allowed to pass out through the lines. Persons to be allowed to pass inward towards Hampton, unless it appears that they intend to go around about, and dodge through to the front. At midnight, Col. Duryée will march his Regiment with fifteen rounds of cartridges on the county road towards Little Bethel, scows will be provided to ferry them across Hampton Creek. March will be rapid but not hurried. A howitzer with cannister and scrapnell to go. A waggon with planks and materials to repair the New Market bridge. Duryée to have 200 rifles. [Sharpe's rifles purchased the day previous are alluded to.] He will pick the men to whom to entrust them. Rockets to be thrown up from Newport News. Notify Commodore Pendergrast (flag Officer) to prevent general alarm. Newport News movement to be made somewhat later than this, as the distance is less. If we find and surprise them, we will fire one volley, if desirable not reload, and go ahead with the bayonet. As the attack is to be by night or dusk of morning, and in detachments, our people should have some token, say a white rag on the left arm.

"Perhaps the detachments which are to do the job should be smaller than a Regiment; 300 or 500 on the right and left of the attack, would be more easily handled. If we bag the Little Bethel men, push on to Great Bethel, and simultaneously bag them. Burn both Bethels, or blow up if brick. To protect our rear, in case we take the field pieces, and the enemy should march his main body (if he has any,) to recover them, it would be well to have a squad of competent Artillerists, regular or other, to handle the captured guns, on the retirement of our main body. Also to spike them if retaken. George Scott to have a shooting iron. Perhaps Duryée's men would be awkward with a new arm in a night or early dawn attack, where there will be little marksman duty to perform. Most of the work will be done with bayonets, and they are already handy with the old ones."

This crude memorandum formed the basis of the official plan, for the first battle for the maintenance of the Republic.

In compliance with instructions, Col. Duryée with the Advance Guard the Zouaves, crossed Hampton Creek at midnight, and advanced upon Little and Great Bethel. Arriving at the former about 4 o'clock in the morning of the 10th, he surprised the Picket Guard of the enemy, who with a mounted

Officer were taken prisoners. While pushing forward towards Great Bethel, he suddenly heard a heavy fire of musketry and artillery in his rear, and supposing it an attempt of the enemy to cut off his reserve, Col. Duryée immediately countermarched in quick and double quick time. Having proceeded about four miles, to near New Market Bridge, his advance reported that the Column from Newport News and the reserves from Fortress Monroe, had mistaken each other in the darkness of the night for enemies, and that an unfortunate engagement had taken place between the 3d and 7th New York Regiments, with considerable loss of life.

Gen. Pierce then called a council of war, and notwithstanding the suggestion by several of the senior Colonels, that the object of the expedition, a surprise, had been defeated by the fatal error of the night, he resolved to proceed. Col. Duryée accordingly again took the advance for Great Bethel, and in compliance with orders previously isued, he burnt Little Bethel, and a large house said to belong to Major Whiting of the Rebel army, as from this, his troops were fired upon as they passed along the road.

On approaching Great Bethel, the enemy opened upon the advance of the Federal troops with artillery and musketry from strong defensive works on the other side of the river. Their position was well chosen, and the Union troops with only one smooth bore six pounder and two mountain howitzers, were engaged with several batteries in a strong position. After an action of three hours, Gen. Pierce ordered a retreat, and the Union forces retired in good order and well in hand. Although the result seemed unsuccessful, the object of the expedition was attained, and the enemy who had been accustomed to annoy our outposts by night attacks, and seize and carry off Union citizens and negroes to serve with their armies, were induced to withdraw their artillery, and retire towards Yorktown the same day. The Rebels numbered about 1800 men under Col. J. B. Magruder, in this affair, which was magnified by them into a great victory It was the first engagement of the Union troops, and caused great excitement throughout the United States. The people and the press appeared to acknowledge it as a defeat, although the conduct of our troops reflected the highest credit upon their valor. It must be acknowledged that the expedition was hastily conceived, and undertaken without Cavalry for reconnoissances, or adequate means for the work in hand. The plans were not mature, and we had not sufficient knowledge of the position and strength of the enemy.

It may not be inappropriate to introduce here an incident before the battle, written by Adj. Stevens of the First Vermont Regiment, and published in the *St. Albans Messenger.*

"Just as we halted to start to the rear, on hearing firing, a rebel scoundrel came out of a house, and deliberately fired his gun at us. The ball passed so close to me that I heard it whiz on its way, going through the coat and pants, and just grazing the skin of Sergeant Sweet of the Woodstock Company The rascal was secured and is a prisoner, and what was done by way of stern entertainment to one of the F F V's. you will hear if I ever live to return. I then with revolver in hand, accompanied by Fifer, approached the fellow's house, having some expectation of an ounce of lead being deposited in my tall body without asking my permission. Without the ceremony of ringing, I entered and surveyed the premises, and found a most elegantly furnished house. I took a hasty survey in search of arms, but finding none, I left the house to overtake our column.

"On reaching the bend in the road, I took a survey of the rear, to see what I might see, and discovered a single soldier coming towards me and waited for him to come up. I found it was Clark of the Bradford Company. Before he reached me, I saw a horseman coming at full speed towards me. On reaching the house he turned in, which induced me to think him a secessionist. I ordered Clark to cover him with his rifle, and revolver in hand ordered him to dismount and surrender. He cried out, 'Who are you?' Answer, 'Vermont!' 'Then raise your piece Vermont, I am Col. Duryée of the Zouaves,' and so it was. His gay looking red boys just then appeared, turning a corner of the road, coming towards us. He asked me the cause of the firing in the rear, and whose premises we were on. I told him he knew the first as well as I did, and as to the last, could give him full information; that the house belonged to Adj. Whiting, who just before had sent a bullet whizzing by me and shot one of my boys, and that my greatest pleasure would be, to burn the rascal's house in payment. 'Your wish shall be gratified at once,' said the Colonel. 'I am ordered by Gen. Butler, to burn every house whose occupant or owner fires upon our troops. Burn it' He leaped from his horse, and I upon the steps, and by that time, three Zouaves were with us. He ordered them to try the door with the butts of their guns. Down went the door and in went we. A well packed traveling bag lay on a mahogany table. I tore it open with the hopes of finding a revolver, but did not."

A match was applied to some clothing, on the table, other fuel was added, and in a few minutes a fire was in progress. The account continues:

"Before leaving, I went into a large parlor in the right wing of the house; it was perfectly splendid. A large room with tapestry carpet, fine piano, sofas, rich chairs with splendid needle work wrought bottoms, what-nots in the corners, and other elegant furniture, together with articles of luxury, taste and refinement, a fine library of miscellaneous books, and upon the centre table lay a Bible and a lady's portrait. The last two articles I took, and have them now in my possession. By this time the Zouave Regiment came up. I joined them, and in a short time came up with our rear guard, and saw a sight, the like of which I never wish to see again, viz: nine of Col. Townsend's Albany Regiment stretched upon one floor, eight of them mortally wounded by our own men."

General Pierce having been relieved, Col. Duryée again assumed the command of all the troops at Camp Hamilton. Upon the disaster of Bull Run, a large portion of his command embarked for Washington by way of Baltimore. On the arrival of the troops at the latter place, Col. Duryée with his

Zouaves occupied Federal Hill, where they constructed one of the most formidable and extensive forts of the kind in the country.

On the 31st of August, the President of the United States appointed Col. Duryée a Brigadier General, and placed him in command of one of the largest brigades in the service, consisting of the 21st Indiana, 3d, 4th and 5th New York, 2d and 5th Maryland, 17th Massachusetts, 7th and 10th Maine, 111th Pennsylvania, 4th Wisconsin, 21st Massachusetts, and 6th Michigan Regiments, Nimm's Massachusetts Battery, and two squadrons of cavalry. These troops were placed under Gen. Duryée for drill and instruction in the science of arms. Few men in the country possess the united influence and skill to raise and discipline so large a body of troops in so short a time, as he had done, and hence his appointment to this important position.

About the first of March, 1862, General Duryée, ardently desiring a command in the field, made the following application.

Baltimore, March, 1861.

"GENERAL MARCY,

Dear Sir: My object in writing to you is to obtain your influence with Gen. McClellan to place me in a position of more activity. I should be indeed happy to be under your immediate command. I have had under my instruction, since the war broke out, twenty regiments of infantry, two batteries of artillery, and three companies of cavalry. I earnestly hope that an opportunity may be offered me to participate with the General, in any of his engagements, and through your kindness hope to be successful in this my application.

"Yours with high Respect.
"A. DURYEE, *Brig. Genl.*"

To this the following reply was received.

"*H. Q. Army Potomac, Washington, Mar.* 12, 1862.
"GENERAL: Your letter, asking to be placed in more active service, has been received. I am directed by General Marcy, Chief of Staff, to say that your application will be laid before the Commanding General at the first opportunity.

" Very Respectfully your obedt Serv't.
" E. A. RAYMOND, *Capt. & A. D. C.*"
"Brig. Gen. A. DURYÉE, *Baltimore.*"

About this time, the plan of the campaign had been entirely changed by the evacuation of Manassas by the rebels, and General McClellan was directed to move upon Richmond by way of the Peninsula. Gen. Duryée made application in person to be placed in command of a brigade in the field, and Gen. McClellan assured him, that he would grant his request at the first opportunity. The commander in chief was at this time embarking his troops at Alexandria, and was upon the point of sailing. On the 20th of March, 1862, Gen. Duryée received orders to report to Gen. Wadsworth, second in command at Washington, and in a few days, through the influence of the latter, he was placed in command of a large Brigade of newly arrived regiments.

CHAPTER II.

ORGANIZATION OF THE BRIGADE.

On the 16th of April, 1862, Gen. Duryée took command of a Brigade formed of the 97th, 104th and 105th New York, 12th Virginia, and 88th and 107th Pennsylvania Regiments, at Cloud's Mills, about two miles from Alexandria, on the Little River turnpike. The 12th Va. and 88th Pa. were a few days after transferred; but the other four remained without change during the period that Gen. Duryée continued in command. These Regiments had but recently arrived in Washington, from the encampments where formed, and the men had every thing to learn concerning the duties of the field, and the vicissitudes of camp life. The change of climate and exposure in tents, had caused considerable sickness, and the Regimental hospital were filled with sick; but as the spring advanced, the wholesome regulations and strict discipline of the camp, with careful attention to its sanitary condition, restored the command to a high degree of health. This Camp of Instruction received the name of Camp Reliance, and was laid out with great care. The tents issued for privates, were of the common A pattern; and from the adjacent camps of the Army of the Potomac, which were left with the tents standing, an additional supply was obtained to meet every suggestion of comfort. The immediate neighborhood of Camp Reliance had been occupied during the preceding winter by Sumner's Division, and every vestige of fencing or other sources of fuel had been consumed, leaving an open country, with here and there a lone family, or more frequently the ruins or foundations of a homestead burnt, or its materials carried off to be used in camp.

The three weeks spent in this location, were diligently employed by Gen. Duryée in drilling and disciplining his Brigade, and in imparting that familiarity with the evolutions of the field, that subsequently carried it through seven battles under his command. The mode of meeting emergencies was practically shown, and the alacrity with which the men were brought into line, by a midnight alarm, gave assurance that the lessons thus taught were well remembered.

On the 11th of May, Gen. Duryée moved by railroad, to Catlett's Station on the front, where he relieved Gen. Hartsuff, and encamped. The 1st Rhode Island Cavalry and Thompson's Battery of Artillery were here annexed to the command. The latter continued in company with the Brigade through all its subsequent marches, being in the same Division, and in battle often in close relation, so that, although not strictly attached in matters of record, a friendly association between officers and men was maintained throughout. The Cavalry soon passed to another command.

Important movements were at this time going on in the Shenandoah Valley. Gen. Banks, after the battle of Winchester, March 23d, advanced up the Valley, following the defeated Jackson to near

Harrisonburg. The command of Gen. Milroy was advancing from the direction of Monterey, and it became an object with Stonewall Jackson, with largely increased forces to prevent the junction of these two armies. If he could capture or disperse the garrison at Front Royal, and get into the rear of Gen. Banks, then at Franklin, or compel him to abandon his works, which were being thrown up at Strasburgh, a most important advantage would be gained. The Union forces under Generals Milroy and Schenck were attacked by Johnson's and a part of Jackson's forces, on the 8th of May, at Bull Pasture Mountain, near McDowell, and obliged to fall back under cover of the night, after first destroying a large amount of Quarter master's and Commissary's stores. The enemy lost no time in placing obstructions between Milroy and Banks, and in making preparations to attack the latter.

Jackson's command could not have been less than 25,000 men, while the forces under Gen. Banks consisted of ten Infantry Brigades of less than four thousand men, with nine hundred Cavalry, ten Parrot Guns and one Battery of smooth bore six pounders.

On the 22d of May, Stonewall Jackson moved down the road from Luray, the advance under Gen. Ewell, and bivouacked ten miles from Front Royal. The object of this movement was to surprise the garrison at that place, under Col. Kenley of the 1st Maryland, and get in the rear of Gen. Banks who was then at Strasburgh. On the evening of the 23d, Col. Kenley was attacked, and those of his command not killed, wounded or captured, escaped towards Strasburgh. The reinforcements that had been hastily sent out were recalled, and the overwhelming numbers of the enemy becoming apparent, Gen. Banks resolved to attempt a retreat upon Winchester, as his only chance of safety. At 3 A. M. on the 24th this movement began, which ended in the arrival of the greater portion of his command, at Williamsport on the Potomac, on the evening of May 25th, by a march of fifty-three miles, in forty-eight hours from the time of the first news of the attack on Front Royal. In this march they met and drove a strong force that had got into the road before them, and fought a vigorous battle at Winchester. During the whole course of their retreat, they were closely pressed by the enemy, yet their loss in killed was but thirty eight, in wounded one hundred and fifty-five, and in missing about five hundred.. They saved all their cannon, and in a train of five hundred army waggons, but fifty five were lost. The ability with which this retreat was managed, reflected the greatest credit upon both officers and men.

The news of this sudden movement excited the liveliest interest throughout the north, and large bodies of Militia were hastily ordered to the field, to meet any attempt at farther invasion. Events were at this time transpiring near Richmond, which demanded a concentration of all the forces that the rebels could command, and it soon became apparent that Jackson could not long remain on the Upper Potomac. It was an object of the first importance, to endeavor to intercept his return up the Shenandoah valley, and no time was lost in ordering a concentration of troops towards Front Royal. The forces under General Fremont already beyond the mountains and those under General McDowell opposite Fredericksburgh, were ordered to effect this object if possible.

Gen. Duryée's Brigade, being at Catlett's, was already many miles nearer the scene of intended action than the remaining forces of Gen. McDowell, and as the tidings of advancing columns of the enemy in the upper valley, the reports of the battle, and news of the Federal retreat and impending danger, came in from hour to hour to the War Department, they were flashed over the telegraph to the commanders in the field, and changed from time to time, with the changing phases of the tidings from the front.

At 11 o'clock P. M. May 23d, Gen. Duryée was ordered to be prepared to move a regiment to occupy Thoroughfare Gap in the morning, as the guard had been attacked at Front Royal and driven off. The regiment was to be accompanied by cavalry, and was to report to Gen. Geary. The balance of the command was ordered to fall back to Bristow.

On the next morning he was directed to leave the forage and supplies at Catlett's for the use of Gen. McDowell's troops. Two columns of cavalry, one battalion of the Rhode Island cavalry of 250 men, and the Virginia cavalry 300 men, were dispatched, and the 104th Regiment N. Y. Volunteers were sent by rail road, with two days rations provided.

Gen. Geary's command when thus reinforced, consisted of a large Pennsylvania Regiment, the

104th, and part of a regiment of Michigan cavalry The 104th arrived at Thoroughfare Gap, on Saturday night May 24th. Gen. Geary's head quarters were then at White Plains, but the next day he moved back. On Monday morning a reconnoitering party went out in the direction of New Baltimore, and returned about noon, having seen nothing. A message was soon after received, that the enemy was moving in large force to cut off their retreat, and Gen. Geary ordered the camp and garrison equipage to be piled, and the troops to march with as little delay as possible. The property was fired by the cavalry and destroyed, at a point just beyond the Gap. The 104th proceeded to Manassas, where it was temporarily detached from the Brigade by Gen. McDowell, and sent to Catlett's, to perform guard duty while the remainder of the Brigade was on the expedition to Front Royal.

On the afternoon of the 24th, a telegram was sent, ordering Gen. Duryée to fall back to Bristow, that night or the next morning, leaving a small force to guard the public stores. On the next morning he was ordered to form a junction with Gen. Geary, and on this day (May 25th), the Brigade was temporarily assigned to Ord's Division.*

The following telegrams were sent on the 26th:

Washington, May 26, 1862.
GEN. DURYÉE,
    at Bristow.

General Shields is here, will reach Catlett's to-

---

* Special Orders 104. Department of the Rappahannock. Gen. McDowell.

day. Keep yourself well informed what is in front of you. Be prepared to fall back on Manassas, and unite with Gen. Geary if threatened by superior force, but do not move until it becomes necessary.

E. M. STANTON,
Sec. of War.

War Department, Washington,
May 26, 1863.

To Gen. Duryée,
at Bristow.

Banks is believed to have made good his retreat with all trains and not much loss to Williamsport. Shield's Division is on the march to Catlett's, and will be there to-day about noon. It is believed Gen. Shields himself is here, and will go down to Catlett's this morning. We still hold Harpers Ferry. Report every thing you hear. We hope to be able to bag the enemy that attacked Banks. Fremont and McDowell are both moving for that.

EDWIN M. STANTON,
Sec. of War.

Washington, May 26, 1862.

To Gen. Duryée.

You will occupy Centreville to-night, with three regiments and a battery.

JAS S. WADSWORTH.

In compliance with this order, Gen. Duryée at once marched, and without halting at Manassas, arrived in the night, during a rain storm, at Centreville. The Brigade there bivouacked, and remained until the 31st of May. The retreat of Jackson was begun on the 30th, and was at once known by the troops before Harpers Ferry. On the 31st Gen. Duryée was ordered to form a junction with Gen. Ord, of McDowell's Corps at Thoroughfare Gap, in order to march upon Front Royal, and intercept Jackson in his retreat up the valley. Pending the march, Gen. Duryée's command was assigned to Gen. Ricketts's Division (June 1st, 1862); and it subsequently remained in this connection through the following movements of the campaign, until after the battle of Antietam.

The march to Front Royal was made under many trying circumstances, and with incidents of the most perilous character. The occasion for vigorous effort was most urgent, and the movement was made with as much rapidity as possible. The men suffered greatly on the first day from heat and thirst. The remainder of the march was made during and in the intervals of drenching rains. Four days were consumed on the march from Centreville to Front Royal, and the latter part of the march was made on a most tempestuous night, and over mountains and rugged roads, a cold rain pouring at intervals in torrents. The advance guard, a company of the Rhode Island cavalry under Captain, Aynsworth, charged on the enemy early in the morning of the 30th of May, completely surprising the guard at Front Royal. The gallant captain was instantly killed,—his body being pierced by seven balls; but his men pressed foward, killing and wounding about fifty of the enemy, taking 185 prisoners, and securing the bridge across the Shenandoah. Seven locomotives and a large quantity of army stores were among the trophies captured.

The rebel force consisted of the Eighth Louisiana, four companies of the Twelfth Georgia, and a body of cavalry, who were so entirely surprised that they had no time either to save or destroy property. The Union loss was reported at eight killed, five wounded, and one missing. Some thirty or forty Union men, who were taken prisoners a week previous, were released. The first infantry that arrived, was Kimball's Brigade of Shields's Division, who reached Front Royal at 11 o clock on the morning of the 30th. A tremendous rain storm began on the 2d of June, and lasted several days; all the bridges on the Shenandoah and Rappahannock were swept away, and the movement of troops became next to impossible. Jackson left Strasburg on the evening of June 1st and pushed with all haste up the valley, narrowly escaping the pursuit, but finally winning the race, after fighting with Fremont at Cross Keys on the 8th and with Shields at Port Republic on the 9th of June. The troops under General McDowell in person, arrived within hearing of the cannonade, but too late to check the movement. An advance was begun, but news from the front gave intelligence that the wary Jackson had escaped. Duryée's Brigade after remaining at Front Royal till the 11th, guarding the town, bridges and fords, returned by rail road to Catlett's Station, at which place, and at Weaverville, they again encamped. The troops from Fredricksburgh belonging to King's Division, returned to their former position.

The army of Stonewall Jackson remained in the upper Shenandoah Valley, but a week after the battle of Port Republic when it marched for Richmond, leaving no forces sufficient for aggressive movements in the interior.* The entire object of the Nothern Campaign was centered upon the rebel capital, for the attack and defense of which the mightiest energies of both parties were now directed.

A new plan of operation was arranged, in which an army was to approach Richmond by the interior routes, with the design of coöperating with the army of the Potomac, then on the Peninsula, but the course of events was eventually turned into a tide of disaster, through the largely increased efficiency of the rebel army, upon the arrival of Jackson. The expedition that was to have approached Richmond from the rear, became in its turn the means of saving the armies under McClellan from still greater reverses, and by drawing upon itself the weight of the enemy's forces, enabled them to w:thdraw in safety for the defense of their own capital, which, by the vigorous efforts of a desperate foe, was in its turn threatened.

* Jackson marched from near Harrisonburgh on the 17th of June, and reached Ashland, 16 miles from Richmond, on the 25th. His three divisions were commanded by Generals Whiting, Ewell, and Winder, and embraced ten brigades and eight batteries.

CHAPTER III.

THE ARMY OF VIRGINIA — ADVANCE TO CULPEPPER — BATTLE OF CEDAR MOUNTAIN.

On the 26th of June, 1862, most of the Union forces in Virginia, and not in the Army of the Potomac on the Peninsula, were organized by an order of the President into a distinct command, named the ARMY OF VIRGINIA, and placed under the direction of Major General John Pope, who had acquired a very favorable reputation from recent successes in the western country.

The Army of Virginia was composed of three corps, viz:

1ST CORPS. The troops of Siegel, which had lately served under Gen. Fremont, of the Mountain Department. Its Divisions were under Generals Schenck, Von Steinwehr and Schurz.

2D CORPS. The troops of Gen. Banks, lately known as of the Shenandoah Department, consisting of two divisions subsequently under Generals Williams and Augur.

3D CORPS. The troops under Gen. McDowell, recently of the Department of the Rappahannock. This corps at first consisted of two divisions under Generals King and Ricketts, with Bayard's Cavalry Brigade. An unorganized force near Alexandria under Gen. Sturgis, preparing for the field was also

ORGANIZATION OF RICKETT'S DIVISION.

attached to this corps, but never joined it for active operations. Reynold's Division of Pennsylvania Reserves, joined the First Corps near Warrenton late in August, and continued with it through the season.

In addition to these bodies of Infantry, there was a proportionate amount of Cavalry and Artillery, and as then organized, one Regiment of Cavalry and four Batteries of Artillery were associated with each Division.

The First and Second Corps were at this time in the Shenandoah Valley, between Winchester and Middleton, the greater portion being nearer the latter place. Of the Third Corps, the first Division under Brigadier General Rufus King, comprising the Brigades of Doubleday, Patrick, Gibson and Hatch, was at Falmouth, opposite Fredericksburgh, and along the rail road to Aquia Creek, at which place he received his supplies. The Second Division under Brigadier General James B. Ricketts,* was at Manassas Junction, and along the Orange and Alexandria rail road to Catlett's, receiving its supplies by that road from Alexandria.

The reported strength of the First Corps was 11,500, of the Second Corps 14,500, and of the Third 18,500, in Infantry and Artillery. The Second Division of the Third Corps, consisted of the following Brigades:

1st BRIGADE, under Brig. Gen. Abram Duryée

---

* Gen. Ricketts was appointed to this Division in place of Gen. Ord, June 19th, 1862, and Gen. Tower was assigned to the Brigade lately under Gen. Ricketts on the same date. (*Special Orders* 144.)

ORGANIZATION OF RICKETTS' DIVISION.

composed of the 97th, 104th and 105th New York, and 107th Pennsylvania Regiments.

2D BRIGADE under Brigadier General George L. Hartsuff, consisting of the 83d New York (9th New York State Militia), 12th and 13th Massachusetts, and 11th Pennsylvania Regiments.

3D BRIGADE, under Brigadier General Zealous B. Tower, and consisting of the 26th and 94th New York, and 88th and 90th Pennsylvania Regiments.

A Fourth Brigade under Acting Brig. Gen. Carroll joined after the battle of Cedar Mountain, and remained a few days. The First Maine Cavalry, Col. Samuel H. Allen, and four batteries of Artillery. Matthews' and Thompson s Pennsylvania and Hall's and Leppein s Maine were also associated with the Second Division of the Third Corps.*

The designation flags were similar to those used in the Army of the Potomac, and the colors that led Duryée s Brigade were therefore blue and white.† Those of each regiment were similar, with the addition of the figure denoting the number of the regiment, according to the date of rank of the colonel commanding.

* These Maine Batteries, belonged to the 1st Regt. Mounted Artillery. The 2 1, Capt. James A. Hall, was from Waldo and Knox counties, and had a Battery of Parrot guns. The 5th, Capt. George F. Leppein, from Cumberland, Oxford and Kennebeck counties, had six Napoleon twelve-pound howitzers.

Thompson had two twelve-pound howitzers and two iron Parrott guns previous to the battle of Bull Run. Matthew's Battery was Co. F. 1st Pa. Artillery, and had six, three-inch Ordnance guns.

† Gen. Orders Army of Potomac 101, March 24th, 1862. The color of the first Division was red, the second blue, the third red and blue vertical, and the fourth, red and blue horizontal.

The Brigade moved on the 5th of July, to the vicinity of Warrenton, Va., where it encamped on a site of great salubrity, a mile east of the town. The rail road was quickly restored to this point; and during the seventeen days that the command remained at this place, immense quantities of army stores were received and forwarded on to Sigel's and Banks' troops then near Sperryville and Little Washington.

The only event of public interest that occurred at this camp, was the death of Col. Zeigle of the 107th Pennsylvania Volunteers, which occurred after a few hours illness, on the 15th. The Brigade honored his memory by attending his remains to the cars, by which they were forwarded to his home in Pennsylvania. The command of the 107th devolved upon Lieut. Col. Van Allen, who at Cedar Mountain, was relieved by Col. T. F McCoy, the present Colonel.

The 97th was at this time under Col. C. Wheelock, but sickness obliged him to remain behind when his regiment marched from Warrenton, and he did not return until two weeks after the battle of Antietam. Lieut. Col J. P Spofford commanded in all the marches and engagements in which the regiment was concerned, until its return to Washington, when he also left on account of sickness, and was relieved by Maj. C. Northrup, who led the March into Maryland, and commanded at the battles of South Mountain and Antietam.

104th was then under Col. J. Rorbach, who at Waterloo, on the last of July, was obliged to resign on account of ill health, leaving Lieut. Col. L. C

Skinner in command. He also resigned on account of an injury, after the battle of Antietam, and was succeded by Col. G. G. Prey.

The 105th was organized and remained under Col. T. M. Fuller, until after the battle of Cedar Mountain when he resigned and was succeeded by Lieut. Col. H. Carroll, who discharged his trust with much intelligence and merit, until mortally wounded at the battle of Antietam. The command devolved upon Lieut. Col. J. W Shedd, who continued in this office, until mustered out by the consolidation of the 105th with the 94th on the 17th of March, 1863. It is due to the regimental commanders here enumerated, that they discharged their duties with intelligence and zeal.

On the 22d of July, the Brigade marched to Waterloo Bridge,* where the whole Division encamped on a hill adjacent to Carter's River, near its confluence with the Rappahannock. There they received the last visit of the paymaster during the year. In six days, the camp was moved about two miles down the Rappahannock to Hart's Ford, where it was formed on the slopes of a hill, which arose by gentle swells to an elevation of five or six hundred feet above the valley From the Brigade Head Quarters near its summit, was presented a magnificent view of the Blue Ridge and other mountain peaks, stretching away to the southwest until lost in the

---

* There was no village at this point. The place derived its name from that of an extensive woolen factory, which had been burned one week before the arrival of the Division by military authority. It belonged to Isham Keith & Son and Dr. Shelton, and had been employed in manufacturing grey woolen goods for the rebel army.

distance. The river had formerly been navigated to this point, by the aid of dams and locks, of which there were twelve between Waterloo Bridge and tide water at Fredericksburgh.

At Hart's Ford, the Brigade was first reviewed on the 18th of August, by Gen. Pope, accompanied by Generals McDowell and Ricketts, with their respective staffs. He passed on, the same day, to Sperryville.

At this period it was known, that the enemy were concentrating a force at Gordonsville, and along the rail road to Orange Court House, with the view of contesting the advance of Gen. Pope. This force began to arrive on the 19th of July, was estimated at from thirty to forty thousand, under Gen. Ewell. The army of the Potomac, after the disastrous events that ended with their arrival on the James River at Harrison's Landing, was no longer in condition for aggressive operations against Richmond, and the enterprising Jackson, as soon as rested from the fatigues of the recent engagements, was at liberty to throw his whole available forces, against the army advancing from the interior. The reputation that he had acquired for vigorous and decisive action, while it gave confidence to his own troops, had to some extent its natural effect upon those against whom he fought. Notwithstanding this, the army of Virginia was in the finest condition,* and confident in their ability to meet the enemy in battle.

* Some exceptions to this statement should be made. Several of the Regiments of the Second Corps were very sickly, and the invalids were soon after sent to a camp hospital at Warrenton

It may be proper to allude to certain measures that had their influence upon events now occurring. In July President Lincoln, as a war measure, issued an order directing the commanders of armies to seize and use any property within the Rebel states which might be necessary or convenient for their several commands. Under this authority, Gen. Pope on the 18th, issued an order, directing that his troops should subsist as far as practicable, upon the country. The owners were to receive vouchers payable at the close of the war, if they could then prove that they had been loyal citizens. Transportation was to be reduced, and villages and neighborhoods laid under contribution for the subsistence of men and horses. The inhabitants within the lines of our army were to be held responsible for all injury to rail roads or other property by guerilla bands, and houses from whence any soldier or train was fired upon, were to be burned. On the 23d, he issued orders that all disloyal citizens within the lines should be arrested, and that those who were not willing to take the oath of allegiance to the United States, were to be sent south of our picket lines, and if afterwards found in our rear, were to be subjected to the extreme rigor of military law. The inhabitants around Warrenton had already with few exceptions taken an oath of allegiance to the rebel government, and protested against the operations of the order, which it is believed they very generally neglected to obey, nor was the penalty in any case

Sulphur Springs, a most salubrious locality about three miles from Hart's Ford. They barely escaped capture, in the subsequent movements of the army.

enforced. Instances may have occurred in which the liberty of subsisting upon the country, was construed into license to plunder, but these violations of law were limited to stragglers from the main army. Gen. Von Steinwehr of the First Corps, on the 13th of July, issued an order directing five principal citizens of Paige County to be held as hostages, and to suffer death, in the event of any of his command being shot by bushwhackers.

These orders were made a pretext by Jeff. Davis, for directing Gen. Lee on the 1st of August, not to regard Generals Pope and Von Steinwehr as soldiers, and therefore not entitled, in case they should be captured, to the benefit of parole as prisoners of war, but that they, or any commissioned officers under them, taken captive, should be held in close confinement, so long as the above orders of the United States should continue in force. The order further declared that in the event of any rebels being executed, by virtue or under the pretext of the above orders, whether with or without trial, or under the pretense of being spies, or hostages, or any other pretense, it should be the duty of the general, commanding the rebel forces, to hang an equal number of Union commissioned officers who might happen to be prisoners of war in their hands.

The prospect of thus being hung as outlaws, had no further effect, than to strengthen our determination not to be taken prisoners of war, yet several officers of this Brigade were by the fortunes of war, thrown into the hands of the enemy, and for a time denied paroles under these orders. Retaliatory executions however occurred on neither side.

Early on the morning of the 5th of August, the Division under Gen. Ricketts crossed Waterloo Bridge, and the next day encamped about two miles northeast from Culpepper Court House, where they formed a junction with Gen. Banks. The Brigade under Gen. Crawford, and a Cavalry force had occupied the town several days before.

The First and Second Corps, had within a few days moved from Middletown, crossed the Shenandoah at Front Royal, and following the west side of the Blue Ridge, had passed through Luray Gap, and approached from the west. The troops under Gen. Sigel, were at this time at Sperryville, about twenty miles distant, and those of the First Division of the Third Corps under Gen. King, were still at Falmouth and Fredericksburgh, holding the crossing at that place, and guarding the rail road to Aquia Creek.

The evacuation of the Peninsula was ordered on the 3d of August, but delays occurred from want of transports and other causes, so that the march did not begin till the 15th. On the 18th of August, Gen. Burnside was ordered to Aquia Creek, and Reno's Division of this corps, subsequently joined Gen. Pope near Culpepper.

The Cavalry attached to Gen. King's Division had in July made several expeditions against the enemy, and succeeded in breaking up the rail road between Gordonsville and Richmond in several places. An expedition of a part of Gen. Banks's Corps, had advanced as far as Madison Court House, but returned without effecting its object. Gen. Hatch commanding the cavalry was therefore succeeded by Gen. Bufort, who was at the head of Gen. Banks's Cavalry at Culpeper when the Infantry arrived.

Such was briefly the condition of affairs when Duryée's Brigade arrived. Stonewall Jackson having been informed that only a small Infantry force was at Culpepper, advanced from Gordonsville on the 7th of August, and on the morning of the 8th, his Cavalry under Gen. Robertson, met the forces under Generals Buford and Bayard, and the latter were forced to retire. It was alleged that some of the Cavalry fell back without sufficient cause, which led to the following order:—

"Head Quarters, Third Army Corps,
 Army of Virginia, near Culpepper, Aug. 8th, 1862.

"The men of the First Pennsylvania and First New Jersey Cavalry, who this day quit their regiments without authority, while it was successfully engaged with the enemy and fell to the rear, straggling even to Culpepper, are to be dismounted in presence of such of the troops of the corps as can be conveniently assembled to-morrow morning, and will be made to serve on foot. Horses being given to the troops for the purpose of aiding them in advancing on the enemy, and not for getting to the rear, theirs will be turned over to those of the Regiments who have shown how to use them, and the surplus will go to the Quartermaster.

"Brig. Gen. Ricketts is charged with the execution of this order.

"By Command of Maj. Gen. McDowell.
 "S. F. BARSTOW, A. A. General."

(Official)

ADVANCE THROUGH CULPEPPER.

At half past two, on the afternoon of the 8th, the long roll was beat in Gen. Banks's Camps and was taken up in those of Gen. Ricketts's Division, bringing the men quickly into line, and ready for the march. It was soon found that the signal was intended only for the troops of Gen. Crawford's Brigade of Gen. Banks's Command,* and they at once advanced, leaving their camps standing. They marched to a point about five miles to the front, and bivouacked near the spot where on the next day, they fought the memorable battle of Cedar Mountain. Duryée's Brigade, with the rest of the Division, proceeded to strike and pack their tents, and in one hour left the ground and were on their march for Culpepper. The transportation and ambulance trains were parked in the suburbs of the town, and the troops marched through, and rested for a time in the open fields adjacent, awaiting orders.

Just before dark the Division formed, and with bands playing and colors flying, took up its line of march towards the enemy. After advancing about two miles, the command halted, and Duryée's Brigade turned into a clover field near the road. Thompson's Battery was brought up and placed in position on a gentle swell of ground, and the troops halted for the night. The General drew up his Brigade in columns closed in mass, and addressed it in glowing and patriotic terms, reminding them that on the

---

* This Brigade consisted of the 28th New York, 10th Maine, 46th Pennsylvania, and 5th Connecticut, and had with it ten pieces of artillery.

morrow they would be engaged in their first battle. He exhorted them to have full confidence in their leaders, and to march on to the field with the spirit of men determined to win: and to fight with the courage that would insure success and victory. Three rousing cheers were given for the General, and the troops laid down on their arms for sleep. It was a mild, clear, moonlight night, and nothing occurred to disturb their rest, until the bugle call of the reveille aroused them to duty, and bade them prepare for action.

In the morning several batteries of artillery went forward, and early in the forenoon, the remainder of General Banks's Corps marched to the front. The day was intensely hot, and the sky, at first clear, became obscured from the dust raised by the moving columns of troops. The batteries accompanying the Division, stood with their horses harnessed, and the infantry piled their knapsacks, ready to move at a moment's notice. Now and then a report of a cannon was heard in the distance, but nothing happened of particular interest until between three and four o'clock, when an active cannonade began near the mountain about four miles distant, and continued until night. From the hillock on which the battery was planted, a fair view of Cedar Mountain was obtained: the bursting shells could be seen, and the rattling volleys of musketry heard. Gradually the thin, level strata of smoke from the battle spread over the field, and the most intense interest was felt about the progress of events, in which all were eager to participate

THE ENEMY'S ADVANCE. 51

At intervals of a few minutes, couriers passed from the field, and trains of ammunition went forward, but no orders came, and the suspense grew painfully intense.

In his official returns General Pope states, that up to five o'clock, General Banks continued to report that he did not think the enemy had sufficient force to make a serious attack, "showing his cavalry ostentatiously, and using his artillery only." The Division of General Ricketts was held in this position, near the junction of roads to Cedar Mountain and Madison Court House, as he was uncertain which route might be selected by the enemy for his main advance.

But whatever might have been the doubt at an earlier hour, it had now become apparent that the enemy, with a heavy force, now known to have consisted of the veteran Divisions of Generals Winder Ewell and A. P Hill, with a strong force of cavalry, under General Stuart, and seven batteries of artillery, the whole under the immediate command of Stonewall Jackson, was pressing upon the single and unsupported Corps of General Banks, which on that day scarcely numbered more than eight thousand men on the field'

It is no small compliment to the brave officers and men of the Second Corps, that the rebel officers, in their reports, claim that they were opposed by " the combined forces of Sigel, Banks and McDowell, numbering at least 32,000 men," and acknowledge their repulse on their left and center in the early part of the action. Their historian says:

"Engaging a force outnumbering two to one, with heavy reinforcements hurrying forward to overwhelm him, Jackson held his ground with that stubborn nerve which had never yet failed to compel unwilling victory to his standard. The enemy had fought hard, but had fought in vain."

At 5 o'clock the drums beat to arms, and Ricketts's Division marched with alacrity towards the front. General Pope with his staff passed soon after, and was received with cheers as he rode forward. At the top of the hill which gave the first prospect of the distant field, General Duryée's Brigade halted, and loaded for the first time with ball cartridges, with the prospect of using them against the enemy. As the column advanced, it began to meet wounded men, and further on the tired and broken fragments of regiments who had been relieved and were passing to the rear. Yet these men, when questioned, spoke hopefully of the final issue of events, and felt assured that the enemy was so crippled that fresh troops would be able to regain the ground they had lost.

General Milroy's Independent Brigade came up the same evening, in advance of Ricketts's, but with these exceptions, no reinforcements arrived until some time in the night. Sigel's corps was all the previous night on the road from Sperryville, and had not yet come up from Culpepper. The troops under King and Reno, were on the way from Falmouth and Aquia Creek, and did not arrive until after the battle.

General Ricketts came up about dark, and halted

in an open field about half a mile from a belt of woods that stretched across the road. Above these woods the top of the mountain could be seen about two miles distant. It has since appeared, that the rebels, although greatly exhausted by the arduous struggle, had determined to pursue General Banks's defeated army to Culpepper, and that Hill's Division, which had been ordered to the front, was cautiously advancing under the cover of the woods when the reinforcements of General McDowell were seen approaching. The moon rendered objects visible for some distance, and the waving lights of our Signal Corps, on a slight eminence in front, gave indication of our near approach. The fields adjacent to the right of our Brigade were filled with ammunition wagons and artillery of Banks's Corps, that had halted for the night in fancied security. The Brigade was drawn up in columns by division, arms were stacked, and fires thoughtlessly kindled by the teamsters for cooking, were blazing brightly. At this moment, an officer rode up in the twilight, and in tones of authority demanded to what brigade and division these troops belonged? This question could scarcely have been asked by one of General Pope's or General McDowell's staff, and there can be little doubt but that the bold question was put by a rebel officer. He had no more than time to reach the woods, when a sudden and terrific cannonade was opened from the mountain, and from a battery in the edge of a field near the woods. A volley of musketry was at the same time fired upon the head of the column nearest the woods. The trains to the right lost no time in hastening out of range, and the Battery of four pieces under Captain Thompson, with the 2d and 5th Maine Batteries, under Capts. Hall and Leppein, were ordered forward to a slight eminence in front.

The Brigade under the orders of its officers held firm, and not a company broke or faltered. The conduct of Gen. Duryée was particularly admired, as with perfect coolness and self-possession he rode from Regiment to Regiment during the hottest of the fire, reassuring the men by cheerful words, and by himself showing an utter disregard of personal safety. He was also successful in rallying two partially stricken Regiments, restoring confidence in their broken ranks, and reducing them to discipline. Most of the shells went over and struck or burst in the field beyond. The Brigade improved the first lull in the iron storm to form, and march by the flank along the road until arriving within five hundred yards of the enemy, when they filed to the right into a low cornfield. The Batteries had in the mean time been brought into position and opened a most vigorous and destructive fire. This fierce cannonade continued till the enemy was silenced. The Brigade lay directly in the line of fire, and heard the shells of both parties screaming over them, as they lay in front, and subsequently in the rear, of their Batteries.

Soon after the first cannonading in the twilight, and after the Brigade had advanced from its first position, a train of ambulances filled with wounded from the field, which had halted just in the rear, was put in motion for a place of greater safety, and for a few moments was exposed to the fire of a section of artillery from the enemy's left. While retreating before this, it met still another volley from a Battery of New York artillery half a mile in the rear. The captain of this Battery, seeing the commotion in front, began firing without orders, alike endangering friends and foes. The ambulance train, which was almost exactly in line, very narrowly escaped destruction by this fire, which continued until Capt. Ball, of Gen. McDowell's staff, fearlessly rode up in the face of the guns, and placed the captain under arrest. Fifteen shells were thrown by these two cannon, with infinitely more peril to our wounded, than to the enemy.

The result of this cannonade, which continued till midnight, was not particularly disastrous to the Union troops. Fourteen of Duryée's Brigade were wounded, one of them severely. Capt. Shurtliff, of the 12th Massachusetts was killed, and several wounded. This regiment formed in line of battle, and delivered several volleys upon advancing cavalry. There was no retreat whatever, and at a later hour in the night the Division moved further to the right, and by early dawn had taken up a position near where they had first bivouacked, in line of battle, and in full expectation that an engagement would be opened in the morning. This terribly grand spectacle, so novel to most of those engaged, left its impressions that other and more fatal encounters have not effaced, and a bright, cloudless moon has seldom shone down upon a scene of more thrilling interest, or upon ranks of more steadfast men.

The enemy's battery near the woods was Capt. Pegram's, supported by Field's Brigade, and their historian says: "The Federal forces were thrown into complete confusion, and scattered in every direction, to escape the shell rained down on them. A desperate effort was made to cover their further retreat, however, and it proved successful. Three of their batteries were soon worked into position; a heavy cannonade commenced; and although a single battery of the Confederates fought the three opposed to it with unflinching nerve, it was finally silenced, and forced to retire with severe loss." While cognizant to the utter falsity of the substance of this extract, we concede the truth of the closing sentence, because our pickets the next day found the bodies of Pegram and several of his men, a dozen dead horses, and abundant traces of broken cannon and caissons on the ground where his Battery had been planted. This officer, while acting as gunner No. 2, and placing his shell in the mouth of the gun, was beheaded by a shot from Thompson's battery, and fell under the muzzle of his piece, with his hand still on the shell. A newspaper correspondent, in narrating these events, says:

"Later in the evening Gen. Pope and Gen. Banks had a narrow escape. They, with their staffs and body guards, were gathered on a hill which gave a good view of the ground, and although it was in front of their lines, retained their position after the lines were formed. As the troops passed, they cheered loudly and repeatedly, and probably drew the rebels attention to the spot, and led them to suspect the General's presence. A battery in the woods near by, opened suddenly upon the hill, and kept up a rapid but inaccurate fire for about twenty minutes. As the shells all went over and exploded in the field beyond, Gen. Pope did not change his position. The battery ceased its fire presently, and the rebel guns elsewhere were also silent. On the left of the hill was an open valley, ascending on the other side to a hill, which half way up was covered with woods. The edge of the woods was not more than a quarter of a mile from the hill where Gen. Pope stood. Very suddenly, while the fire was everywhere still, a battalion of rebel cavalry dashed from the cover and charged down the hill at a gallop, discharging their carbines as they came. Generals, staffs and escorts mounted and started without much delay, riding straight for their own lines, but scattering to avoid the rebel fire. But the moment the rebel cavalry came in sight, the nearest infantry (12th Massachusetts) ignorant or careless of their General's position, opened with a volley along the whole line. It checked the rebels, and did not kill many friends; but for four or five minutes, the cross-fire under which the generals and all were compelled to pass was rapid and hot. The sight of a sheet of flame from the line whose protection we sought, and the whiz of friendly bullets was a little startling; but there was nothing to do but to keep on, for the fire continued, and the longer we waited the worse it would be. Two of Gen. Pope's body guard were killed, and one wounded. Gen. Banks was severely injured by a runaway cavalry horse, which struck him on the side, but he kept in his seat, and remained in the field all last night and this morning. Col. Ruggles, Gen. Pope's chief of staff, had his horse shot under him. Col. Morgan, aid-de-camp to Gen. Pope, and Maj. Perkins, Gen. Banks's chief of staff, both had bullets through their hats."

Gen. Pope in his official report to Gen. Halleck on the 13th, says:

"The engagement did not fairly open until after six o'clock, but for an hour and a half was furious and unceasing.

"Throughout the cannonading, which at first was desultory and directed mainly against the cavalry, I had continued to receive reports from Gen. Banks that no attack was apprehended, and that no considerable infantry force of the enemy had come forward.

"Yet towards evening, the increase in the artillery firing having satisfied me an engagement might be at hand, though the lateness of the hour rendered it unlikely, I ordered Gen. McDowell to advance Ricketts's Division to support Gen. Banks, and directed Gen. Sigel to bring his men upon the ground as soon as possible.

"I arrived personally upon the field at 7 P. M., and found the action raging furiously. The infantry fire was incessant and severe.

"I found Gen. Banks holding the position he took up early in the morning. His losses were heavy

"Ricketts's Division was immediately pushed forward, and occupied the right of Gen. Banks, the brigades of Crawford and Gordon being directed to change their position from the right and mass themselves in the centre.

"Before this change could be effected it was quite dark, though the artillery fire continued at short range without intermission.

"The artillery fire at night by the 2d and 5th Maine Batteries, in Rickett's Division, of Gen. McDowell's Corps, was most destructive, as was readily observed next morning in the dead men and horses, and the broken gun-carriages of the enemy's batteries which had been advanced against it.

"Our troops rested on their arms during the night in line of battle, the heavy shelling being kept up on both sides until midnight.

"At daylight the next morning the enemy fell back two miles from our front, and still higher up the mountain. Our pickets at once advanced and occupied the ground.

The fatigue of the troops from long marches and excessive heat made it impossible for either side to resume the action on Sunday The men were, therefore, allowed to rest and recruit the whole day, our only active operation being of cavalry on the enemy's flank and rear.

"Monday was spent in burying the dead and getting off the wounded. The slaughter was severe on both sides, most of the fighting being hand to hand. The dead bodies of both armies were found mingled together in masses over the whole scene of the conflict.

"The burying of the dead was not completed until dark on Monday, the heat being so terrible that severe work was not possible.

"On Monday night the enemy fled from the field, leaving many of his dead unburied and his wounded on the ground and along the road to Orange Court House."

The report of Gen. McDowell says:

"The cannonading of the 8th had been resumed on the 9th, and was kept up more or less throughout the day. The reports from the front sent in to me, and from Gen. Banks to your headquarters, (where, by your direction, I had been throughout the day,) were to the effect that the enemy did not yet seem to be in great force, showing his cavalry somewhat "ostentatiously" and using his artillery only; and these reports continued to be of this character throughout the day, and gave the assurance the enemy would not be able to bring up his main force until our army should have been sufficiently concentrated and got in good condition for battle.

"Gen. Sigel's Corps having arrived at Culpepper after a forced march, much of it during the night previous, and being reported without provisions and not in a condition to immediately follow Gen. Banks, by your order I directed subsistence to be given to Gen. Sigel's men from my supply train, and instantly took Ricketts's Division, accompanied by you, to the front to join Gen. Banks without waiting to follow Gen. Sigel, as had been before ordered.

"When the order was given to me to take Ricketts's Division to the front it was not known Gen. Banks had attacked the enemy, or that he purposed doing so, or that the enemy was in sufficient force to attack him; but the cannonading having become more continuous, I was sent forward as a precautionary measure, and to allow Gen. Sigel's men some rest. When between two and three miles from Cedar Mountain, we began to meet the evidences of the battle which Gen. Banks had fought at its base—stragglers, singly and in groups, and soon companies, battalions and batteries, moving to the rear. Gen. Banks had left the position where he had drawn up his troops, and moved them forward to attack the enemy, not believing him to be in any great force, and found him stronger than he supposed, outnumbering greatly his own corps, and had been driven back after a gallant, severe, and bloody contest.

It was now dark, and under the assurance of Gen. Banks that the remainder of his corps were in the front of a narrow strip of wood which extended across the road, that a brigade was still on a hill to the right of this wood, and that this brigade and the right of his line, which was said to be intact, would be drawn towards and strengthen his centre, which had suffered most, I was ordered to place Ricketts's to the right and front; this was done by posting Tower's Brigade with two batteries, Shippen's and Thompson's, on the knoll to the right of the wood, Carroll's Brigade connecting the left of Tower's line with the woods. Hartsuff's and Duryée's Brigades in second line, with Hall's and Thompson's Batteries in reserve. But while making these dispositions and moving forward in column to do so, the enemy, following up the retreat of Gen. Banks, established a battery beyond the woods before mentioned and opened on the head of my column, and soon after coming through the woods with infantry, cavalry and artillery, established another battery on the knoll where you had just before made your headquarters, after your conference with Gen. Banks and others. This battery fired on the second line of Ricketts's Division, and until the battalions in mass were placed under the shelter of the rolling ground took effect on Hartsuff's Brigade. Quickly the batteries in reserve, under the direction of that most valuable officer Maj. Tellson, chief of artillery, Hall's 2d Maine and Thompson's 2d Maryland opened on the enemy. It was dark and only by the flash of the enemy's pieces could they see where to direct their aim, but soon by a rapid and well-directed fire, they silenced the enemy's batteries and forced them to withdraw, leaving some of their officers and most of their horses dead on the ground. The fire of the enemy's infantry from the woods was mostly at Carroll's Brigade, which suffered from it before his men could be got into position in the front line.

"The hot reception given the enemy by Ricketts's Division caused the enemy to fall back during the night to their former position on and near Cedar Run Mountain, some three miles.

"Finding Ricketts's Division too far to the front

and right it was drawn over during the night by your direction, to the right of the position you had directed Gen. Sigel to occupy.

"On the morning of the 10th (Sunday) nothing was done by either army beyond a few dropping shots, and we remained in position, under arms, awaiting a renewal of the attack, which was not made, there being only one false alarm of a movement on our right flank.

"The 1st Pennsylvania cavalry, under Col. Owen Jones: the 1st New Jersey cavalry, under Lieut. Col. Karge, (Col. Wyndham being a prisoner of war on parole;) the 1st Rhode Island cavalry, under Col. Duffie, and the 1st Maine, under Col. Allen, all under Brig. Gen. Bayard, had been engaged in the battle before we came up, and I am assured by your chief of cavalry, Brig. Gen. Roberts, who was present, they performed good service, not only before but during the action. Gen. Bayard, who had himself rendered most valuable service, speaks warmly of a charge made about 5 o'clock, P. M. by that gallant old soldier Maj. Falls, 1st Pennsylvania cavalry, who led his battalion against the enemy's lines and charged completely through them.

"All the regiments above named, and especially the Pennsylvania and New Jersey, had severe duty to perform in holding the enemy in check.

"There are two officers of my staff—aides-de-camp—who are deserving of especial mention in connexion, Capt. Leslie and Capt. Howard Stockton. Having had no officers of topographical engineers, they were placed on this duty, and were constantly in front exerting themselves with a zeal and intelligence that accomplished much for the army, and especially for the advance."

Gen. Milroy, commanding an Independent Brigade, reported as follows:

"I have the honor to submit the following report of the movements of my command since the departure from Woodville, Virginia, on August 8, 1862:

"At 9 o'clock, P. M., my brigade taking the advance of the corps, started in the direction of Culpepper, arriving at the place about 5 next morning. At 5 P. M. of the same day received orders to march immediately in direction of Cedar Mountain, from which direction heavy firing had been heard all the afternoon.

"I again took the advance. Having marched some three miles, and finding the road blocked up by ambulances and stragglers from the battle-field, I started ahead with my cavalry detachment, (three companies of the 1st Virginia,) leaving my infantry and artillery to make the best of their way to the front. Arriving about 9 P. M. at the front, and finding everything in confusion, I ordered my cavalry into line, under the protection of the woods nearest the enemy, and advanced alone to reconnoitre. Fifteen minutes had scarcely elapsed when a battery of the enemy suddenly opened with great precision upon the remnant of Gen. Banks's corps, posted on my right. The enemy's fire had been directed by several large fires, burning brilliantly among Banks's Batteries. The result was a general stampede, artillery, cavalry, and infantry retreating in the greatest disorder. I endeavored to rally them at first without success, but finally succeeded in arresting a battery or two and some cavalry, which I brought back to their old position on the road, at the same time throwing my cavalry across on the same side. Shortly after one of Banks's Batteries, having retreated to a safe position, commenced, to the left of the road and behind us, responding to the enemy's guns, the firing ceased in about fifteen minutes.

"Meanwhile, fearing that my brigade, two regiments of which had been thrown across the road to stop the terrified mass in their headlong retreat, might be delayed too long, I despatched one of my aids to hurry it forward—to push before them all of the retreating column possible. They immediately proceeded forward, and after much labor I succeeded in encamping them, near 2 A. M., in the position first selected in the evening. Having posted pickets at a suitable distance in our front, I allowed the men to rest on their arms."

Early the next morning, Sigel's Corps had come up, Banks's Corps had been withdrawn, and the troops under Milroy and McDowell lay in line of battle, their skirmishers thrown forward to the edge of the woods, along which there was some picket firing. A few shells were thrown into the woods without visible effect, and the Sabbath passed away without further events. From officers who then lay wounded on the field, we learn that throughout the day the enemy were industriously employed in burying their dead, and otherwise concealing their losses, which could not have been less than ours, for the fire of our artillery had been terribly destructive. The slight and imperfect manner in which these burials were made, indicate the amount of work they had to do, and when we advanced a few days after, parts of the bodies of their dead were already exposed, as they lay on the surface, with a few shovels full of earth thrown over them.

On the 11th, the Union dead were buried under a flag of truce, by parties detailed for the purpose, and allowed to pass the enemy's lines, as far as to Cedar Run, beyond which line they were not permitted to come. Gen. Milroy in reporting these events, says:—

"*Sunday, 10th.*—Still holding a position in advance of the corps, I threw forward a line of skirmishers, with a sufficient support, along my whole front. They found the enemy's skirmishers, supported by their whole force, strongly posted in the woods about 2,000 yards in front of us. Here they skirmished until about noon, the enemy occasionally firing upon them by companies. Whenever this occurred, I would send a few shells among them, causing their sudden withdrawal. During the afternoon my skirmishers drove the enemy from the woods, following them some three-fourths of a mile. About 4 P. M. sent out my cavalry to reconnoitre, and, if possible, to allow the ambulances to bring off some of our wounded. In this they were quite successful, bringing off about one hundred. The cavalry had in the meanwhile approached within 300 yards of the enemy's lines without drawing their fire, and having ascertained their position withdrew to our lines.

"On the morning of the 11th, it being determined to take the dead and wounded from off the field, I was ordered to advance my Brigade and cover the ambulances and working parties. I accordingly sent forward my three companies of cavalry, followed by my infantry The cavalry, upon arriving at the outskirts of the wood, halted, finding ahead of them a strong cavalry force under the direction of General Bayard.

"I then rode forward, followed by several ambulances, which I sent back loaded with wounded. About an hour had thus elapsed, when I was informed a flag of truce had been sent in by the enemy, and at the same time received a request from Gen. Bayard to attend a conference with the rebel Gen. Stuart relative to a cessation of hostilities for the purpose of attending to the dead and wounded of both parties. An armistice until 2 o'clock, P. M. was finally agreed upon, but was afterwards, by mutual consent, extended to the evening."

Jackson's army retreated on the night of the 11th to beyond the Rapidan, and Sigel's Corps was ordered forward to Robinson's River, his lines extending from Madison Court House to the river. In this retreat he left many of his dead and wounded on the field and along the road, and many of the latter were brought in by the Federal surgeons and sent to Culpepper and Washington. A large portion of the First Division of McDowell's Corps arrived from Fredericksburgh on the 11th, and encamped about three miles south of Culpepper, while the remainder proceeded to Catlett's. Gen. Reno's Division of Burnside's Corps united with Pope's army on the 14th.

Ricketts's Division marched on the 15th to a point on the Rapidan, six miles beyond Cedar Mountain, near Robinson's River, where it encamped. The rebel pickets were but a short distance beyond, and Col. Carroll commanding the Fourth Brigade was wounded by their sharpshooters while on the outposts. His command devolved on Col. Thorburne of the 1st Virginia Regiment. Several of the cavalry were also wounded. No fires or lights were permitted in our camp after dark, and on the 16th the ambulances and ammunition trains were sent back to beyond Cedar Mountain.

CHAPTER IV

RETREAT FROM THE RAPIDAN—BATTLES OF RAPPAHANNOCK STATION AND THOROUGHFARE GAP.

Reports showed that Jackson was being reinforced, and the withdrawal of McClellan from the Peninsula enabled the whole rebel force around Richmond to be thrown against the Army of Virginia. It was a matter of the first importance with the enemy, to do this before Pope could form a junction with McClellan, from his new base of operation at Aquia Creek or Alexandria. An expedition of Union cavalry to Louisa Court House captured Gen. Stuart's Adjutant General, and among the papers found, was a letter from Gen. R. E. Lee, in which this purpose of the enemy was fully confirmed. Our spies also reported that the enemy were preparing to move in heavy columns behind the hills with the evident intention of crossing below, and of gaining the rear of Pope's army No time was lost in anticipating this movement.

On Sunday, August 17th, Duryée's Brigade, in common with the Division, marched at two o'clock in the afternoon, and proceeded leisurely through the cornfields and across farms, about five miles, passing on the right of Cedar Mountain to a bivouack near Calvary Church. The army telegraph was this day extended to the Rapidan, and a heavy force was employed in rebuilding the railroad bridge, doubtless with the view of keeping up appearances of an advance to the latest possible moment.

On the 18th the army was mustered, and work on the bridge was pressed with energy till nightfall. The officers of the several regiments towards evening were privately informed that a retreat would begin that night at eleven o'clock, and that the Rappahannock was to be reached and passed before a permanent halt would be made. The camp-fires were to be built and allowed to die down as usual, and nothing was to transpire to inform any spies, who might be lurking near, of the intended movement. Late in the evening, the bridge was destroyed by a party detailed for the purpose, and several men were seriously, and one fatally, injured by the falling timbers.

Early in the afternoon, all the trains were sent forward. The men were silently aroused a little before eleven o'clock, and with the greatest stillness and order marched towards Culpepper, but after going about two miles were halted to allow the immense trains which covered the late battle field to move on. But two or three thousand army wagons, each with four horses or six mules, are not easily managed, and eight hours elapsed before the last was under way, filling all the parallel roads of the country that led towards the Rappahannock. The privacy of the march was soon revealed by long lines of fires built by the roadside, as the night was chilly, and miles of blazing fences would have shown to the least observant, our position, numbers, and intentions.

It was eight o'clock on the morning of the 19th before the Brigade could march. It then proceeded in perfect order along the road by which it came, resting at convenient intervals. From Culpepper, the route led along the roads near the railroad to Rappahannock station, where the Division crossed on the railroad bridge late in the evening, after a march of twenty-two miles. No enemy was seen, and a stranger would have observed nothing unusual, excepting now and then an army wagon burning by the wayside, where it had broken down. The last of the railroad trains passed in the afternoon, and the more valuable portions of the military stores had already been forwarded to Manassas, where they were subsequently destroyed. About eighty Union wounded, not in condition to be removed, were left in charge of five surgeons, and an ample supply of medical stores. These wounded as they recovered were sent to Richmond, and many were there exchanged and sent North.

The citizens of Culpepper, who were very generally disloyal, had through the whole time of occupation, evinced their Southern preferences in many offensive ways, and now could scarcely conceal their joy at the retreat. The women, especially, well knowing that their sex secured personal immunity, watched in groups from their doors and gateways, the passing columns, and often made derisive comments, or insulting remarks; yet private property and personal rights were carefully respected by our troops. Along the railroad track, great numbers of contrabands were constantly seen passing on towards Washington and freedom. Singly, in pairs, in groups, by families and in squads of ten and twenty, the dusky throng pressed forward, sometimes with a horse harnessed to a cart laden with their little ones, and the sum total of their wealth, often carrying their children upon their backs, and always with the inseparable bundle. Their women were often dressed in the finery of deserted homes, and the grotesque scenes presented on this day and the following were novel and often amusing.

The army trains which had crossed at various fords, were the next day moved back to Catlett's and parked. Sigel's Corps marched from Culpepper through Jefferson to Warrenton Sulphur Springs, Banks and McDowell to the railroad crossing, and Reno through Stevensburgh to Kelly's Ford. The rear was covered by the cavalry, and the last of these under Gen. Bayard, spent the night of the 19th near Culpepper, and fell back the next morning, skirmishing with the rebel advance, and giving time for our entire forces, with their trains, to cross.

Having concisely stated the movement of the Union forces, it may be interesting to quote from a writer to the *Charleston Mercury*, an account of the rebel advance:

"*August* 19*th*, *near Orange Court-House.*—Orders issued from headquarters for the army to move forward in light marching order. At daylight, everything in motion toward the Rapidan, which is ten miles distant. The enemy in front and on this side of the river. Longstreet at the head of his column. The Federals back rapidly as we advance, our front and their rear-guard having one or two slight skirmishes. Jackson is moving towards the left, probably with a view to flank the enemy in case of a stand.

"*August* 20.—Army crossed the Rapidan, the water thigh deep. Scene exciting and amusing. Nearly the whole day thus occupied.

"*August* 21.—The enemy in close proximity, and we have to move cautiously. Longstreet's Corps is in front. From a hill on the other side of the Rapidan we have a magnificent view for miles. Three columns—long, black winding lines of men, their muskets gleaming in the sunshine like silver spears—are in sight, moving in the direction of Fredericksburg, or down the opposite bank of the river. More skirmishing in front. Good many stragglers by the wayside, but they are generally broken-down soldiers, and trudge slowly along in the tracks of their comrades. An attractive part of the procession is the baggage trains wending their way in the rear of the army. Thousands of wagons are in sight, and between the stalling of trains, the shouting of drivers, and the chaotic confusion which emanates from the motley mass, no man can complain of the *ennui* of the march.

"Nothing can be more picturesquely beautiful than the bivouac at night. Thousands of troops line the woods on both sides of the roads for miles. Camp fires are glimmering in the trees, muskets are stacked along the edge of the forest, and the men are disposed in every conceivable manner. Some are rolled up in their blankets, and already dreaming away the fatigues of the day; some are sitting around the camp fires watching the roasting ears, and discussing the 'coming events which cast their shadows before,' and some are among the trees, moving to and fro in the gray film of smoke that has arisen from the myriad fires and rests upon the earth. We live upon what we can get—now and then an ear of corn, fried green apples, or a bit of ham broiled on a stick, but quite as frequently do without either from morning until night. We sleep on the ground without any other covering than a blanket, and consider ourselves fortunate if we are not frozen stiff before morning. The nights are both damp and cold.

"*August* 22.—To-day another busy scene. The army resumed its march at daylight. Longstreet's twelve brigades moving towards the Potomac on the right and Jackson on the left. The latter has passed the Rapidan Station on the Virginia Central Railroad, and is pressing on north-east of Culpepper. Several small skirmishes have taken place on the front, and eighty or ninety prisoners went by on their way to the rear. Among the Yankees captured by Jackson were two men, who, as soon as they fell into our hands, commenced to ask after their old comrades in the artillery company. An inquiry being instituted, they confessed that eight months ago they were soldiers in our army, but that, being tired of service, had deserted and joined the ranks of the enemy. Without further ado, the

General ordered them to be hung to a tree, which was done in the presence of a large portion of his army."

The main body of the rebels under Gen. Lee crossed the Rapidan at Raccoon Ford, and Jackson's forces at the railroad crossing.

At 1 o'clock, P. M., on the 20th, from the hills on the north bank occupied by the artillery of Ricketts's Division a long line of cavalry skirmishers were seen approaching in the distance, and the scattering fire of carbines came every moment nearer, while clouds of dust showed the movements of columns of rebel troops approaching. In the rear of our skirmishers was a few army wagons, and the last of the negro throng, hastening towards the bridge.

Our whole force was withdrawn, except two regiments of Hartsuff's Brigade, and a section of Matthews's Battery, which were posted in some old earth works, on two small hills on the south side, one about one hundred and fifty yards from the road, and as many from the river, and the other four hundred yards from the road and six hundred from the river. A heavy cannonade was heard on the left, but nothing occurred in front, and the Brigade lay supporting batteries through the day. Gen. Sigel, after crossing at the Springs, marched down and joined McDowell's troops on their right. Some skirmishes occurred on the 21st across the river, in which the Union troops captured seven horses and seventy cattle.

Gen. Pope's orders were imperative to hold the line of the Rappahannock at all hazards, and until he could be reinforced.* The stream at that season could be crossed at many points, and the utmost vigilance was necessary to prevent the enemy from crossing with overwhelming force. Gen. Pope in view of the probability that large additions would speedily be made to his army, resolved to march over and attack the enemy on the south side, and with this view, early on the 21st, sent out a strong working party, under Major Huston, of the Engineers, consisting in part of men detailed from Dur-

---

* *U. S. Military Telegraph, from War Department,*
Washington, August 18, 1862.

To General POPE.—I fully approve your movement. I hope to push a part of Burnside's forces to near Barnett's Ford by to-morrow night, to assist you in holding that pass. Stand firm on the line of the Rappahannock till I can help you. Fight hard and aid will soon come.

H. W HALLECK, General-in-Chief.
GENERAL POPE.

U. S. Military Telegraph, from War Department,
Washington, August 20, 1862.

To General POPE.—I have telegraphed General Burnside to know at what hour he can reinforce Reno. Am waiting his answer. Every effort must be made to hold the Rappahannock. Large forces will be in to-morrow.

H. W HALLECK, General-in-Chief.
GENERAL POPE.

U. S. Military Telegraph, from War Department,
Washington, August 20, 1862.

To General POPE.—I have just received Gen. Burnside's reply General Cox's forces are coming in from Parkersburg, and will be here to-morrow or the next day. Dispute every inch of the ground, and fight like the devil till we can reinforce you. Forty-eight hours more and we can make you strong enough. Don't yield an inch if you can help it.

H. W HALLECK, General-in-Chief.
GENERAL POPE.

yée's Brigade to construct a bridge about half a mile above the rail road crossing. At about 10 o'clock, a vigorous cannonade was heard up the river, and during the forenoon, the enemy crossed with cavalry and infantry, but were driven back by King's Division. The temporary bridge gave a shorter and sheltered communication with the position on the south bank, and the remainder of Hartsuff's Brigade with Thompson's and Matthews's Batteries were passed over. The old rebel earthworks, thrown up to face northward, were made available for their new use, by fatigue parties, who worked through the night previous. During the day an active cannonade was continued along the river both above and below, and heavy masses of Rebel troops were seen passing in the distance. It was however quiet at the rail road bridge, where Duryée's Brigade remained supporting Hall's Battery. A shower of rain occurred towards evening, and it rained at intervals in the night.

The morning of the 22d found our position on the south bank strengthened. The cannonade began at 5, 30 in the direction of the new bridge, and continued at intervals through the day, at times increasing with fearful violence and then subsiding.

The enemy was seen approaching directly in front of the rail road bridge at 11, 30 in great force, and the batteries along the north bank opened upon the advancing masses with activity. A mounted officer, apparently in command, was seen to fall, when the enemy fell back, and the field became quiet.

In a telegram dated at 9, 15 P. M. Gen. Pope informed Gen. Halleck, that reports were received of the enemy's crossing above, and on the road to Warrenton, while still in force on the Rappahannock. He found it necessary either to fall back and join Gen. Heintzelman's forces behind Cedar Run, or cross and attack the enemy at daylight. He preferred the latter, but left the decision with the Department, and an answer approving this alternative was returned.

The night closed in dark and rainy, and the morning of the 23d dawned upon a river swollen six or seven feet above its recent level. The bridge by which the First Division with Generals Reno and Reynolds had orders to cross and attack the enemy, was swept away, and its timbers lodging against the rail road bridge, endangered its safety also. The brigade and batteries on the south side were withdrawn in safety, and the enemy at once came forward and occupied their late position. A furious fire was opened against our troops, but was answered by our four batteries, and the sharp shooters, and the Division as it lay in the rear, slightly sheltered by the slope of the hill, met with some loss.

As the swollen river rendered the fords impassable, for a few hours, and as the enemy were reported to have crossed above, the whole command withdrew at about ten o'clock, after first destroying the rail road bridge; Companies C and G, of the 26th N Y Regiment were detailed to remain behind, and burn the depot and village of Rappahannock Station, to prevent the timber of the houses from being used to rebuild the bridge. This service was performed under the supervision of Major Jennings, without loss, although the enemy brought up their cannon to the river bank and opened upon them at short range. The ruin was effectual, and when accomplished the companies rejoined their regiment near Warrenton.

Having sent the sick and wounded to Bealton Station and thence to Alexandria, the Command marched to meet the enemy, then supposed to be in force near Warrenton. From the top of a hill the Brigade of Gen. Duryée halted on the march in the twilight, a magnificent view was obtained of a cannonade going on between Sigel's forces and the enemy, on opposite sides of the river. The flash of the guns of both parties could be distinctly seen, followed in about half a minute by the report.

The command halted in the edge of a piece of woods for the night, and the men exhausted by their recent labors, laid down without suppers and were soon asleep. The 104th Regiment was detailed as a guard to Gen. Pope's head quarters.

On Sunday the 24th, the corps started in the gray of morning, and upon approaching Warrenton marched to the left, and formed in line of battle on the road leading to the Sulphur Springs. They soon advanced down the road, and halted in a beautiful grove, attached to an aristocratic mansion. The troops were entirely destitute of provisions, but they here found an abundance of green corn, which, with fresh meat obtained by foraging, supplied their present wants. A barn full of grain furnished forage, and a building stored with tobacco, was eagerly explored by those who had long been deprived of this luxury. The Division of Gen. Reynolds, joined McDowell's Corps at this place on the 24th, a cannonade was heard to the right, which was understood to be between General Banks's troops and the enemy, at or above the Sulphur Springs, or Sigel's at Waterloo Bridge.

On the 25th, the Division remained in the grove till afternoon, and during most of the day an active cannonade was going on up the river. Columns of smoke from houses set on fire by the artillery were seen in the distance, and ammunition trains went forward down the road which led to the Springs, about two miles further on.

At four o'clock on the afternoon of the 25th, the Brigade received orders to move two and a half miles, to a new position on the turnpike, leading from Warrenton to Waterloo Bridge. It was understood that the destination that night would be the latter place, where Sigel had imperative orders to force his way across the Rappahannock at daylight.*

* WARRENTON JUNCTION. *August* 25, 1862—9.30 P. M.
You will force the passage of the river at Waterloo Bridge tomorrow morning at daylight, and see what is in front of you. I do not believe that there is any enemy in force there, but do believe that the whole of their army has marched to the west and northwest. I am not satisfied either with your reports or your operations of to-day, and I expect to hear to-morrow, early, something much more satisfactory concerning the enemy. Send back and bring up your provision trains to your command, but no regimental trains or baggage of any description. You will consider

PREPARATION FOR AN ATTACK.

The direction of the march led across fields traversed by ditches, and separated by stone walls, which allowed no vehicle to follow, and it became necessary to send the ambulance train by a different route. A mistaken order, to follow a train of ammunition waggons, passing down the road towards the Springs was given. The error was discovered but the message countermanding this order was not received, and the surgeons in charge, with the entire medical property of the Brigade, and every medical officer of the four regiments present, with their attendants, and several invalids, were led into an adventure full of extreme peril, and attended with incidents which will be remembered for a lifetime.

The train followed slowly down, to near the Springs, and thence by a narrow and difficult road, which led over the hills, past the spot where the head quarters of our Brigade had been located in the encampment of Hart's Ford. But before reaching the foot of the hill, which by a long ascent, led past the old brigade head quarters, it became apparent that something was wrong. Tedious delays were interrupted by the hurried movement of ammunition wagons coming from the opposite direction, and going to Milroy's command at the Springs. Every thing was forced aside to give room for their passage, and a movement among several batteries posted on the hill in front, gave evidence that the condition was at least critical. It finally became

this a positive order, to be obeyed literally. You will communicate with me by telegraph from Warrenton.

JNO. POPE, Major General Commanding.

certain, that the ambulance trains must give precedence to six or eight batteries of artillery; and that the road in front was held by the enemy in force. To return was impossible, as the road was encumbered, and there remained no alternative but to explore a path across the fields and through the woods, over a broken and unknown country to the Waterloo pike.

From the summit of the hill, the opposite banks less than a mile distant, and the valley between, were glowing with a thousand camp fires of the enemy. The evening was still and starlight, and as the night advanced, a thin veil of fog and smoke, lay in the valleys and bottom lands. Turning at right angles from the road at the highest point of the hill, the trains of artillery and the ambulances slowly followed the pioneers, now winding down a deep valley, or crossing a sharp gully, and climbing a steep that would scarcely be attempted by daylight; then following a farm road a short distance, and feeling the way through meadows, orchards and cornfields, often halting for teams to double, in drawing a cannon from a ditch, or waiting for a wall to be leveled, or a road to be cleared through the woods, the painful march progressed, and not until the day began to dawn, did the train explore its way over the three miles of rugged country that ended on the turnpike. Cavalry guides were stationed at different turns, to direct those who followed, and it is believed nothing was lost or left on the way.

Upon reaching Warrenton soon after sunrise, it

was ascertained that the Brigade had been ordered back to its position on the previous day, where the ambulances rejoined the command before noon. A movement was soon after again ordered across to the turnpike, where it lay in line of battle till the afternoon of the 27th. While at this place, a scanty supply train came up, with barely sufficient for the present want, and at once returned to Warrenton Junction.

So effectually had the enemy masked his movements, that in a dispatch dated at 3, 20, P. M. on the 26th, Gen. McDowell expressed great uncertainty, and suggested several theories, conceiving a probable movement into the Shenandoah Valley, &c. It was only *certain* that heavy bodies of troops had passed up the river, but whither and for what purpose he could only ascertain by a cavalry reconnoissance which he had ordered under the direction of General Buford.*

At 2 o'clock on the 27th, the Brigade received orders to march, and leisurely proceeded up the turnpike to Warrenton. The troops began to observe that something unpleasant had happened. They passed a wagon loaded with grain and ammunition which was being burnt, and before reaching Warrenton, were halted and told that they must use every ounce of their rations with the greatest economy and care. In fact, it now became apparent, as already mistrusted, that the enemy in great force, under Stonewall Jackson, had got in the rear, with a force estimated by General Pope at

* Official Report of Pope's Campaign, p. 198.

twenty five thousand men, and cut off communication from Washington, and supplies. The road was to be opened by their valor, and every thing gave assurance that a desperate conflict was approaching. At this very moment, the feeble guard at Manassas Junction, was yielding before Jackson, and as the evening advanced, the sky towards the north east was lit up with reflections of burning trains and depots filled with army stores. A distant cannonade heard in the afternoon in the direction now our front, is since known to have been the battle between General Hooker and the rebel General Ewell, at Bristow and Kettle Run.*

Let us briefly digress, to follow the movements of the army trains that had preceded from the Rapidan, and were parked in the vicinity of Catlett's, during the battles on the Rappahannock. A portion of King's Division with a few of the 1st Michigan Cavalry, and some of Gen. Sturgis's command were in their vicinity, and along the rail road from Manassas Junction eastward. On the evening of August 21st, during a shower of rain, the trains were attacked by a cavalry force that had passed through Warrenton. Apparently well informed of the location and defences, they fell upon General Pope's personal baggage, siezed his valuable papers and several thousand dollars in money, and de-

* This action began about four miles south of Bristow, and Ewell was driven back to Kettle Run at Bristow Station, where he made a stand at dark, and rejoined Jackson before morning. The loss on each side was about three hundred and fifty in killed and wounded. The rail road was torn up and bridges burned in several places —*Pope's Official Report, p.* 17.

stroyed seven waggons.* A vigorous resistance was made, especially by Gen. Gibbons's guard, and the shower prevented them from setting fires. The train of Duryée's Brigade was across a small stream suddenly swollen by the rain, and thus saved from attack.

The sick were left in churches at Warrenton, and on the 27th placed upon cars and sent towards the Junction, but returned that night. After passing two or three times over the road, they were at length removed by wagons from Bristow to Fairfax Station, and thence by cars to Alexandria.

The Brigade marched through Warrenton about sunset on the 27th, under orders to reach Gainesville that night.† The troops under General Sigel had marched in the morning, on the turnpike towards Centerville, and had arrived at Buckland Mills in time to save the bridge over Broad Run, that had been fired. His corps reached Gainesville that night. We was followed by General Reynolds, King, and Ricketts, in the order above named. The corps of Gen. Banks in this movement followed the wagon trains from Warrenton Junction to Centreville without meeting with obstructions, as the enemy had

---

* One who was present thus describes the attack. "About 7. 30, the leader of the attacking party rode up to the guard of Gibbon's Train and said "stack your arms, run your wagons together and burn them; the Rebels are upon you." The guard replied by firing, and the leader's horse fell wounded, upon the leg of its rider, thus holding him a prisoner. The assailants were repulsed, leaving ten dead horses and five prisoners, of whom two were wounded. One was killed on the spot."

† Official Report of Gen. Fitz John Porter's Court Martial, p. 102.

fallen back, with the exception of Gen. Sigel's train,* and the ambulances. There were no wagons but those laden with ammunition on the road, but this was so encumbered by artillery and troops that progress was slow, and the delays frequent and tedious. The night at first starlight became overcast, and as it grew late, stragglers were seen in great numbers, as they had fallen out on the roadside to cook their suppers and to rest. The temptation presented by these cheerful fires, and the thoughts of hot coffee and sleep were too strong for many of the wearied and worn out soldiers to resist. Availing themselves of the darkness, and the shelter of bushes, many slipped out of the ranks unobserved by their officers, until their regiment had passed and then joined the groups before the fires. The Division pushed on to a short distance beyond New Baltimore, where it bivouacked an hour after midnight. The straggling of this night was fearful, yet early in the morning, nearly or quite all came up and rejoined their regiments.

Let us here notice the recent movements of the enemy:

Stonewall Jackson on the 25th had marched from the Rappahannock towards Jefferson, but as soon as out of sight of the river turned to the right through Amissville, crossed at Hinson's Ford, and continued on by way of Orleans to Salem. Thoroughfare Gap was reached and passed on the 26th, before our advance arrived, and the trains and stores at Manassas were in flames, before our army had

* Gen. McDowell's statement in review of evidence before Court of Inquiry, p. 45.

time to realize the extent and true character of his movement, so completely had it been covered by a cordon of Stuart's Cavalry. This force composed of Jackson's old, A. P Hill's, and Ewell's Divisions had marched with a celerity that has few parallels in history, and necessarily left behind it all its supplies, depending for support upon green corn, and such as the impoverished but willing population along the route could furnish. They were worn down with fatigue, and far in advance of the main body under General Longstreet, which was said to embrace the Divisions of Anderson, Jones, Kemper, Whiting, and Evans. A quick and vigorous movement, on the part of General Pope's forces in the rear, and those expected from Alexandria, should have crushed this army before it could be reinforced, yet from reasons before the public, and in no way attributable to General Pope, this result was not realized, and the tide of fortune favoring the enemy, soon drove our shattered armies within the defences of Washington.

At half an hour before midnight on the 27th, the following order was drawn up by Gen. McDowell, at Buckland Mills:

"It being understood that a large division of the enemy under Longstreet left Salem at 4. P. M. for the enemy's position in the direction of Manassas through Thoroughfare Gap, and is now on the march, the following preliminary movements of the left wing of the army will be immediately made:

Major General Sigel's corps will, without delay, be concentrated at or near Haymarket and Gainesville. A division of their corps will be left at Buckland Mills, to operate against the flanks of the enemy or march to Haymarket as shall be found most expedient. King's and Ricketts's Divisions will march to Gainesville, and start at 2 o'clock A. M. to attack the enemy's position in the direction of Manassas. This attack will be supported under the provision of the General Order from Head Quarters of the Army of Virginia, by the command of Maj. Gen. Heintzelman now at Greenwich, and which will be on the right of the attack."

Pending the delivery of this, a dispatch was received from Gen. Pope at Bristow Station, ordering a march to Manassas Junction, as Jackson, Ewell, and Hill, were between that place and Gainesville, where a rapid movement would it was hoped, enable our forces to capture the whole. Reno was directed to march from Greenwich, and Kearney who was in his rear, was ordered to march to Bristow. Early on the 28th, the following order was issued:

"*H. Q. Third Corps, Reynolds's Camp*.
August 28th 1862.

"GENERAL ORDERS, No. 10.

"1. Major General Sigel will immeditely march his whole Corps on Manassas Junction; his right resting on the Manassas rail-road.

"2. Brigadier General Reynolds will march on the turnpike, immediately in the rear of General Sigel, and form his division on the left of General Sigel, and march upon Manassas Junction.

"3. Brigadier General King will follow immediately after General Reynolds, and form his Division on General Reynolds's left, and direct his march on Manassas Junction.

4. Brigadier General Ricketts will follow Brigadier General King, and march to Gainesville; and if, on arriving there, no indications shall appear of the approach of the enemy from Thoroughfare Gap, he will continue his march along the turnpike, form on the left of General King, and march on Manassas Junction, and in case one is threatened, he will form his Division to the left and march to resist it.

The Head Quarters of the Corps will be at King's Division.

By command of
    Major General McDowell.

The march was resumed by Ricketts's Division at eight o'clock on the morning of the 28th, and continued on the turnpike towards Gainesville. The inhabitants informed our troops, that a large rebel army (Jackson's) had, two days before, crossed the turnpike near this place, and we observed that the rails of fences had been piled, so as to allow of the free movements of troops in battle. At a quarter past nine, a cannonade was heard directly in front, and continued at intervals through the day.

A little beyond Buckland, the Division turned to the left, and winding its way across the fields and by country roads, came out on the turnpike leading through Thoroughfare Gap. It was understood that this movement was occasioned by a dispatch from Jackson, intercepted on its way to Longstreet, urging him to hasten up through the Gap with all possible speed. The diversion of Ricketts's Division to oppose this advance, would if successful, enable the remainder of General Pope's army to meet Jackson unsupported, and it was hoped secure victory to the Union arms.

The column of General Ricketts came out on the turnpike at Haymarket about four miles from the Gap, and at once marched forward to meet the enemy who were reported as coming through in overwhelming numbers. Col. Wyndham's first New Jersey Cavalry, had been sent up early in the morning, and by cutting down trees, had done something towards obstructing the advance. The cavalry forces under Generals Buford and Bayard, were stationed near Haymarket, but with this exception, there were no troops within supporting distance of General Ricketts's Division. General Buford with his cavalry, had the day previous approached Longstreet's forces between Salem and White Plains, beyond the Gap, and forced them to deploy, and Duffield's Rhode Island Cavalry had been sent up to watch the road between White Plains and Thoroughfare Gap to prevent the enemy from falling upon the rear of our column on its march from Warenton.

Some of our troops left their knapsacks at Haymarket, but Gen. Duryée's Brigade retained theirs to within a mile of the Gap, where they halted and piled them near the edge of a wood. The Division then advanced, the third brigade under Col. Stiles of the 83d N. Y leading, supported by the First and Fourth brigades, the Second being held in reserve.

The road was so obstructed by fallen timber that some delay was occasioned, and the enemy had in the mean time advanced so as to hold the strongest position, and their infantry were able to lie concealed until the front ranks were at short range. An active engagement presently begun, and was continued from about 3 o'clock till night. The heaviest loss fell upon the Third brigade, and especially upon the 11th Pennsylvania under Colonel Coulter, in which twenty were killed and thirty wounded. Duryée's Brigade in this engagement supported Thompson's Battery, at first on the right, but afterwards to the left of the road leading through the Gap.

The enemy used little or no artillery, and was held in check until nightfall, when General Ricketts learning that a heavy force of infantry was coming through Hopewell Gap, on his right, and that he was also threatened on his left, took up his line of march towards Gainesville, after first halting to take up the knapsacks that had been left in its rear, and to bring off its wounded from the hospital it had established near the scene of conflict.* Upon reaching Haymarket it was learned that a cavalry engagement had occurred during the afternoon, while the Division had been fighting in the Gap, and that the enemy had been repulsed.

* Thirty-nine wounded (one a rebel) were brought off, of whom two died before reaching Gainesville. They were subsequently taken on to Manassas, where after the battle of the 30th, they fell into the hands of the enemy, but finally found their way through to Alexandria. It is believed that none of the wounded were left on the field.

The Division bivouacked in Gainesville late in the evening, under circumstances of extreme peril. In front, was Jackson's army, whose artillery had thundered at no great distance through the day, and close in the rear was the overwhelming force of Longstreet, which now had nothing to obstruct its advance, and might come up at any hour of the night, and fall upon our wearied troops, exhausted with hunger and hardship.

Yet nothing occurred to break the slumbers which even in the midst of danger, stole over our men as they lay down on their arms, in battle array. With the first dawn of morning on the 29th, the Division marched by an obscure road to the right, that led eight miles across the country towards Bristow, cautiously advancing with the cavalry and artillery in front and rear, and every moment expecting to meet the enemy who was known to be near in great force. While thus marching, a heavy cannonade was opened at no great distance to the left, in the direction of Groveton, and apparently within two miles. It was afterwards reported by rebel prisoners, that our column passed within range of their concealed batteries, and that they were only prevented from opening upon it by their ignorance of the strength of our forces.

The march continued in perfect order and without incident, until half past seven in the morning, when upon reaching the summit of a gentle slope, we saw spread before us the plains around Bristow, covered with Union troops, and long trains of wagons coming quietly in from towards Catlett's. The enthusiasm of the men found expression in cheers, as they now felt assured, that the enemy was on one side only. They were willing to meet the rebel horde, but wished to do this in open contest, and with even chances.

At a quarter before nine o'clock in the morning, the advance of Longstreet's army, consisting of seventeen regiments of infantry, a battery of artillery, and five hundred cavalry, marched through Gainesville.

CHAPTER V

BATTTLE OF BULL RUN—RETREAT TO THE DEFENCES OF WASHINGTON.

The Brigade drew a short allowance of rations, and rested a few hours near Bristow, where the unburied dead gave evidence of the recent encounter of Hooker and Ewell. A vigorous effort was being made to restore the rail road bridge over Kettle Run to enable the trains laden with sick and stores from Warrenton to pass, but the measure failed, and the next day these trains were destroyed.* The march was resumed before noon, along the road to Manassas Junction, where the brigade halted at the point of divergence of the rail roads for some time, within sight of the ruins of the trains which had been burned two days before by the rebels.

At the Junction, the Division came up with Gen. Fitz John Porter's Corps, which lay along the Manassas Gap rail road. Since early morning, the thunder of artillery to our left, had given knowledge that the battle was progressing between the

*August 30, 1862—6, 30. P. M.

Destroy the public property at Bristow, and fall back upon Centreville at once. Destroy all the rail road property. Your troops at Bristow will withdraw through Brentsville. Your troops at Manassas and between there and Bristow will withdraw to Centreville.

By command of Major General Pope.
        GEO. D. RUGGLES, Colonel and Chief of Staff.
GENERAL BANKS.

ARRIVAL ON THE FIELD.

advance columns of General Pope and Stonewall Jackson, and every one felt assured, that the opportunity would soon be given to meet these hostile forces, now beyond doubt heavily reinforced by the reserves of Longstreet. At about four o'clock, orders came, directing the Division to march for Sudley Church on the extreme right, where a most vigorous resistance had been made, on the previous evening, and great danger was apprehended. Passing Porter's Corps, the command advanced about five miles, along the road, and across fields that led to the Warrenton Turnpike, at the celebrated Stone House, so often mentioned in the first battle of Bull Run. Half a mile before reaching this point, the Division from the summit of a commanding eminence, gained the first view of the opposing forces, and our appearance was welcomed with cheers by the wearied troops, as they lay in line of battle on the slopes across the valley. It was then almost sunset and the sky, nearly cloudless, was tinged with a reddish hue, as the setting sun cast its last rays upon the battle field. Along a range of hills parallel with that on which we stood, but of lower elevation, was the front line of batteries, with infantry resting on the slopes behind, and their colors floating in the breeze. Beyond these, and a mile or less from them, were the batteries of the enemy, and at intervals of a minute or two a puff of smoke and flash of light, followed in a few seconds by the report, gave intimation that some inviting object had presented itself within range of cannon. To the rear, on each side and to great distances were scattered the camp fires of our reserves and ammunition trains, and the red flag on every building along the way, gave notice of its use as a hospital for wounded.

The march of this evening had led across a country dry and barren, the houses nearly all deserted, and the fields still waste and unenclosed as when desolated the year before by contending armies, or by the improvidence of troops encamped through the winter in their vicinity The soil is red and sterile, and the surface uneven and often cut into sharp ravines, or swelling into low hills covered with stinted cypress, or overgrown with bushes. Yet the thirsty men sought in vain for water along the ravines, as it had all sunk into the porous shales, and the few wells of the country had been rendered useless. The route to the battle field led past the wooden camps which had been occupied the winter before by Toombs's and Wilcox's rebel brigades.

The troops of Ricketts's Division bivouacked near the Stone House, within range of the enemy's shells, and early the next morning marched to a point about a mile to the right, entered a piece of woods, and presently came to some slight obstructions, and met the enemy's skirmishers. Passing the former, by moving obliquely to the right, the Brigade formed in line and advanced by the front, across a rail road cut, and to a short distance beyond, the whole line, being still in the woods except the right which came out into a clearing and corn field. The enemy before them were the troops of Stonewall Jackson, chiefly Hood's old brigade of Texans and a Louisiana brigade. Skirmishers were sent out into the field, and an irregular firing began, with an occasional volley from the regiments on the left. While in this position, the enemy were seen to bring up a battery about a third of a mile distant, upon an eminence, and soon began a brisk cannonade, which continued about twenty minutes. In the mean time the rebel skirmishers opened a fire obliquely from the left, which occasioned some loss. As the Brigade had no artillery support, and was already in advance of the general line of battle, orders were given to about face, and fall back to a position behind the rail road cut. By some means the 107th Penn'a, on the extreme right, with a part of the 97th, did not get this order, and remained for some time in advance, but rejoined the rest of the brigade as it formed a new line in the rear.*

The shells of the enemy burst over and beyond the Brigade, while on its advanced line, and occasioned some loss, in wounded. Among these was General Duryée, who was wounded in the hand, and received a contusion from a shell, but remained in command throughout the day. The enemy's artillery had the range of the ambulances in the rear of the woods, and compelled them to withdraw, with such of the wounded as had been brought out from the front. These, with other wounded brought from the field in the early part of the day, were sent to a camp hospital, which the

*The knapsacks of the men were piled near the first line formed and left when the Brigade fell back. Upon the General's calling for volunteers to go and recover them, Sergeant Francis J. Brennan of Co. H. 97th N. Y. Vol's, stepped forward, and with some thirty others performed this service in the face of a severe fire, and without loss.

Medical Director had established on Bull Run, between Manassas Junction and Centerville.

During the forenoon, the Brigade took a new position a little further to the right, in the edge of the woods which they had entered in the morning, the right wing still fronting as before, but the left turned to face the enemy on the left. The angle thus formed was in the 97th Regiment. Thompson's Battery of four pieces was brought up and planted on the left of the line, in front of the 104th Regiment. This movement was made to check the tendency which had several times been shown by the enemy, to attack from the left.

On a swell of land now in front of the left wing, and on the general line of battle, were about a dozen pieces of artillery, which had been served at intervals through the day. The troops far to the left, about five o'clock in the afternoon, began to be pressed by an advance of the enemy in overwhelming numbers, and the roar of battle, as it was heard advancing further and further, gave indication that our forces were being driven from that part of the field. Soon after, the rebels were seen marching in columns by regiments, and in perfect order, directly up to the batteries on the eminence, and although our artillery made fearful havoc in their ranks, and many were seen to fall, yet the lines closed up the vacant places, and kept steadily on, until within a few yards of the guns, when with cheers they charged upon, and captured them. While this charge was being made, heavy masses of infantry were approaching through the woods, but their presence was not noticed, on account of the darkness and smoke of the battle which the wind drifted into the woods, until they came within close range. They then opened a destructive fire upon the Brigade, and a charge was seen at the same time approaching Thompson's Battery, from the left.

Before this attack on the front and flank, which was fast closing upon the rear, it was useless to stand, and the Brigade made a hasty retreat, obliquely to the right, and thence by a circuitous route, towards the Stone Bridge, where the greater portion crossed after dark. Some crossed Bull Run above the bridge, and were captured by the rebel cavalry who had gained the rear at this point. Thompson saved but one of his guns. Most of the men brought off their arms and knapsacks, and a few of the wounded came off. The rest were necessarily left with the dead on the field. Several of those too badly wounded to be moved were robbed by the enemy, and left, but the second day after were brought off under a flag of truce.*

Early in the afternoon the second and third Brigades of the Division had been sent to the left, under General Tower, with two batteries, to resist the

---

* Among those who were conspicuous on this as on o'her occasions, in their efforts for the relief of our wounded, was the Rev. William T. Campbell, chaplain of the 107th Pennsylvania Regt. who here remained some ten days, a voluntary prisoner with the enemy. He had provided from private means, a light wagon stored with supplies for sick and wounded men, which at Cedar Mountain had proved a most timely resource, but this was subsequently separated from the command, by an inexorable order of General Pope, which denied the right of way to all vehicles not belonging to the Government.

attack being made in that quarter, and did not rejoin the command until the day after. Their loss was very severe, and their spirited leader was dangerously wounded. So uncertain are the fortunes of a battle, that the cessation of firing which occured about noon along the whole front, had led the generals in command to believe, that the enemy were in full retreat, and orders were issued to the several Corps, directing the movements that were to be made by them in the pursuit. General Heintzelman's Command, to which Ricketts's Division had been attached for this occasion, was to follow the road to Sudley Spring, and thence to Haymarket, but the first step brought them upon the enemy's skirmishers and it became apparent, that instead of retreating, they were receiving large reinforcements and were preparing to attack with overwhelming masses.

After crossing Bull Run, the Brigade met with no further annoyance from the enemy, and the next morning reached Centreville.* A little over a mile to the rear of that place, the command halted in the vicinity of its wagon train, to gather its scattered forces, and gain a little much needed rest. It here drew rations, of which the men were extremely in want, and was allowed a few hours of such repose as could be gained without shelter in a drenching rain. But even this relief was of brief duration, for the enterprising enemy now flushed with victory, seemed anxious to make the most of his success, and on Monday September 1st, the

* See Appendix.

second day after the battle, he was found to have pushed his columns northward to the Little River Turnpike, and to be advancing upon Fairfax Court House in our rear. On the evening before, a party of Stuart's Cavalry with artillery, had succeeded in reaching a point near the junction of the roads within a mile of Fairfax, and had thrown shells into a passing train of wagons and ambulances, but without doing serious damage. The wounded at that place, were sent off during the evening to the rail road station, and thence to Alexandria, leaving the village deserted by every one, excepting the provost guard.

On the afternoon previous, the guard at this place had received orders to halt every vehicle that passed towards Washington, and see that each was filled to its capacity with wounded men. No others were allowed to ride, and this rule was most rigidly enforced, to the disgust of a large number of Department clerks, who misled by a premature telegram of victory, had gone out to the battle field, to tender their valuable services in nursing the wounded. But few got beyond Centreville. About sixty of the more enterprising fell into the hands of the enemy, and the remainder, foot-sore and weary, worked their way back to Alexandria. On the first of September, the troops around Centreville fell back towards Fairfax Court House, and late on the afternoon of that day was fought the battle of Chantilly.* Duryée's Brigade on this occasion lay on

---

* The following order was issued by Gen. Pope to Gen. McDowell at noon on the 1st of September, and was executed promptly.

" You will march rapidly back to Fairfax Court House with

the extreme right, and was in line of battle, but not engaged. A terrific thunder storm occurred during the fight, adding sublimity to the scene, but like most of the dramatic incidents of war, ending in misery. The troops were exposed through the night to a cold, drenching rain, and their nearness to the enemy, who were known to be still passing to the right, rendered fires altogether inadmissable. Seldom have the weary hours of darkness worn away more heavily, and never was daylight more welcome than to the men on this occasion. They now had the privilege of building fires, and in their cheerful glow, soon forgot the miseries of the previous night. Such are the lights and shades of a soldier's life! Often called upon to endure hardships and danger, he becomes familiar with suffering and death, yet with elastic vigor, he feels the first impress of returning cheer, and resumes his duties with renewed energy.

The Brigade held its position to the right of the Little River Turnpike and on the front line of battle, supporting a masked battery, and every moment expecting an attack. As the tendency of the rebel movement had for several days been towards our right, it seemed probable that an attack if made would be from that direction, but skirmishers who were sent out a mile to the front returned with the

your whole Division. Assume command of the two brigades now there, and immediately occupy Germantown with your whole force, so as to cover the turnpikes from this place to Alexandria. Jackson is reported as advancing on Fairfax with twenty thousand men. Move rapidly."

The few tents that had been put up near Centerville were destroyed.

report that no indications of the enemy were observed, and about ten o'clock, the line of march was resumed towards Washington. The movement was conducted with the greatest regularity and order, all the trains being sent on before. Banks's Corps marched by the Braddock Road and Annandale to Fort Worth; the Corps of Franklin and Hooker followed the Little River Turnpike toward Alexandria; Heintzelman's Corps took the Braddock road to Fort Lyon: the Corps of Porter, Sumner and Sigel, that to Vienna and the Chain Bridge, and McDowell's Corps marched by the Turnpike to Annandale, and thence by Fall's Church to Hall's Hill. There the brigade under General Duryée arrived late in the evening of the second of September, weary and exhausted with hardship and hunger,—with wasted numbers but unabated courage,—repulsed but not broken in spirit; and although saddened by the loss of many brave comrades left unburied on the field, still hopeful in the final issue of event.

The regiments that had wintered in front of Washington, returned to the ruins of their former camps, now overgrown with rank weeds,—as the wounded bird unable to migrate, might seek her summer nest amid the falling leaves of autumn: and it was sad and mournful to observe their meagre ranks, as they stacked their arms in the familiar streets, and cleared away the rubbish from spots still fresh with memories of their dead.

The cloud of war cast its shadows over the north, but new sacrifices and new efforts were destined to turn back the invasion that east and west threatened to sweep over the land.

The Generals commanding our Brigade and Division, enjoyed to the fullest extent the confidence of their troops. General Duryée had won a place in the hearts of his men, by an untiring devotion to their welfare, and had gained their fullest confidence and respect, by evincing a personal bravery that seemed to know no fear, when it led in the path of duty.

General McDowell in reviewing the services of his Corps during the month of August says:—

"In compliance with general orders, the corps fell back to Hall's and Upton's Hills, in front of Washington. Here the campaign ended. If it had been short, it had been severe. Beginning with the retreat from Cedar Mountain, seldom has one army been asked to undergo more than our men performed. With scarcely a half-day's intermission, the 3d Corps was either making forced marches, many times through the night, and many times without food, or were engaged in battle. These fatigues were most severe towards the last, when, on account of the movements of the enemy, we had to be separated from our supplies, and many generals, as well as privates, had no food, or only such as could be picked up in the orchards or cornfields along the road. In all this, the patience and endurance and general good conduct of the men were admirable. To fight and retreat, and retreat and fight, is a severe test of soldiership. This they did for fifteen days; and though many broke down under the fatigue and exposures, and many straggled from the ranks, the troops as a general thing, behaved most creditably, and even to their return to the lines in front of this place, though they were sad at seeing their numbers so much diminished by hardships and battles, which had availed them nothing, and were tired and reduced from marching and fasting, they preserved their discipline, and it is an abuse of words to say they were either demoralized or disorganized.* * * * *

General Ricketts, who at Cedar Mountain and at Rappahannock, was under my immediate Command, and rendered valuable service with his Division, speaks in high terms of the gallantry of Brigadier Generals Duryée and Tower, both at Thoroughfare Gap and in the battle of the 30th, in which the former was slightly, and the latter severely wounded."

CHAPTER VI.

THE CAMPAIGN IN MARYLAND—BATTLES OF SOUTH MOUNTAIN AND ANTIETAM.

General McClellan on the 2d of September, was placed in command of all the troops lately under General Pope, for the defences of the Capital, and on the 7th the latter was, at his own request, relieved and transferred to the Department of the North West.

Meanwhile the rebel armies, having now nothing to oppose their long cherished plan of an invasion of Maryland, pressed forward on the 3d to Drainsville, on the 4th to Leesburgh, and the day following to the Potomac; fording the river at and near Point of Rocks, they rapidly advanced upon Frederick City and from thence sent out their videttes many miles in all directions, spreading the greatest alarm throughout the north, and causing the most urgent preparations to be hastened to meet the formidable invasion.

The Army of Virginia, (now merged in the Army of the Potomac under General McClellan), had scarcely time to rest, much less to repair the fearful waste of equipage and clothing occasioned by their recent services, when the summons came, "fall in" for another march, to meet the victorious enemy on the soil of Maryland.

On the evening of September 6th, just as the men were preparing for another night's quiet rest, a luxury to which they had so long been strangers, orders were received to march immediately. The route led towards Georgetown, where the Brigade crossed on the Aqueduct bridge at midnight, and without halting, passed through Georgetown and Washington. The route led along the Avenue and L street, to Seventh street, where it turned due north up the turnpike towards Rockville. The troops marched with alacrity until they crossed the river, but the temptations of the town proved too strong for some who had long been a stranger to the comforts of civilization, and as the column receded from the city, straggling became fearfully prevalent, both with officers and men. Some had expected that the Brigade would be assigned to the defence of the forts around the Capital, but the head of the Division continued on without halting till daylight. Most of this march was at a quick step, and such was the effect, that when the first halt was made, eight miles from the city, the regiments scarcely averaged fifty men present in the ranks, the remainder being scattered along the road.* During the three hours that this halt was

*It was afterwards said that Gen. Ricketts was not present in this night march, being detained on business. The mounted orderlies who carried the flag, appeared not to *know* or not to *care* at what rate they were marching, and some one besides the *men*, should share the blame of this shameful affair. Gen. Duryée was sensible of the great impropriety of such a headlong course, but could only follow his leaders. It was simply an impossibility for exhausted men to keep up with mounted cavalry made, great numbers came up, and a short distance beyond, the Division halted for the day, entirely without food, and both officers and men eagerly seeking from the unripe corn and fruits of the country, some relief from the gnawings of hunger.

On the 7th the command marched but four miles, and halted in a highly cultivated region. The enclosed fields, gathered harvests, ripening fruits, and barns filled with plenty, brought back the memories of home, and the scenes of luxury and comfort appearing on all sides, presented a strange contrast, to the barren and wasted fields of Virginia. From many a family group by the wayside, the soldiers were greeted with cheers of welcome and tokens of hospitality, that gave assurance of loyal sympathies and heart-felt prayers for success. The star spangled banner floating from the roofs of houses, or waved by gentle hands, became a common and welcome object, on the succeeding days of the march, inspiring the troops with enthusiasm and giving promise of victory

There was another cause that went still further in producing confidence and hope among the men. A charge in Corps and Department Commanders had been made, and although History will do justice to the merits of those who had been recently superseded, it was enough for the troops to know that they had been again and again beaten. The causes of these disasters were then not known, and although now, we may be able to find in them sufficient reasons for the sad reverses that had driven us across the Rappahannock and the Potomac, it is due to truth that we should here record the lively satisfaction with which this portion of the late Army of Virginia, was told, that they were henceforth to be led by McClellan.

Partial supplies arrived on the 8th, and an order was received reducing the transportation to the least possible allowance, depriving officers of personal baggage, and the field hospitals of every pound of stores that could be spared beyond their present wants. The Division marched to near Mechanicsville on the afternoon of the 9th, and on the 11th continued through Brooksville to where the road came out on the great National Road at Cooksville. The command was on the right of the main Army of the Potomac, which was at this time advancing by the parallel roads nearer the river. Halting near Cooksville for muster and inspection of arms and equipage, the Brigade marched at noon on the 12th, towards Frederick City, and as it advanced, the reports of distant cannon, that had been of late so familiar, were again heard in the advance, giving notice that the enemy was again met. This firing was in the environs of Frederick City, from which the enemy was retreating, leaving his sick to our care, and bearing off the ill gotten plunder of private stores. On the afternoon of the 13th we marched twelve miles along the National Road and just at night crossed on the splended Stone Bridge over the Monocacy Here the Division bivouacked in the fields a little below the bridge, with orders to march at the earliest appearance of daylight.

Throughout the morning, and at intervals during the day, an active cannonade had been heard in front, and a rumor prevailed that the enemy had retired some seven miles along the road, and was holding the mountains over which we must pass before reaching the Potomac.

On the morning of the 14th the reveille beat at three o'clock, but we did not get under way until a little after sunrise. The morning was beautifully serene, and as we advanced, the spires of Frederick City appeared in fine relief, with mountains in the back ground. A cannonade so distant as to be barely audible was heard due west, for a few minutes, about sunrise. Vast bodies of troops were concentrating at this place, and the active movements on all sides gave notice of vast preparations to meet the great events so soon to pass before us. As the Brigade entered the city, its principal streets were thronged with troops. Hundreds of Union banners floated from the roofs and windows, and in many a threshold stood the ladies and children of the family, offering food and water to the passing troops, or with tiny flags, waving a welcome to their deliverers.* Patriotism, with these good peo-

---

* The contrast of this welcome, is thus related by a rebel correspondent, as he described the reception of Jackson's army a few days before: "The advance of our army arrived on Friday night [Sept. 5th], and we are now encamped around the town. Martial law has been proclaimed, a Provost Marshall appointed, and a strong guard of our men patrol the streets to preserve order.* * There is yet, little openly expressed enthusiasm. As Jackson's army marched through, the houses were mostly closed, and from between the window blinds, the citizens could be seen anxiously peering, as if they expected to see a crowd of bugaboos intent upon nothing but rapine and slaughter."—*Daniel's Life of Gen. Jackson*, 197

ple was no abstract theory, but a living fact, intensified by the recent contrast of Southern Chivalry in their midst, which while robbing them of their property, added insult to injury, by tendering in mock payment, the trash not worth its weight in rags.

It was the Sabbath day, and like good Christians they had closed all places of business; yet notices of "Sold out," "Closed up," and like evidences of the end of trade, chalked on the doors, gave reasons to suspect, that piety was not altogether the motive which led to this strict observance of Sunday

The troops made but a short halt in the town, and continued on towards the enemy, passing by the way the traces of the skirmish which we had yesterday heard in the distance. A heavy cannonade towards Harper's Ferry, told of a contest there pending, of whose chances and results all were anxious, but of the disgraceful issue of this engagement, we were not informed until the day following. Our road led up over the Catocton Hills, and as we arrived on the summit, and gained a view of Middleton Valley and South Mountain beyond, a new interest was given to the scene, by the distant view of the cannonade going on eight miles in front. Groups of citizens of both sexes, from the city, were watching the battle that was progressing, and every few seconds, a puff of light blue smoke, a little white cloud suddenly appearing in the sky, and a report, showed the position and activity of rebel batteries, along the top of the mountain, and those of the union troops on the hills below.

At Middleton, the academy, the churches, and private houses were open to receive the wounded, of whom many had already been brought in, the earnest kind hearted ladies of the village, were industriously ministering to their wants, bringing in their best bedding and pillows,—sheets for bandages, and dainty food for feeble men. With the tenderness of sisters, these angels of Mercy, watched by the side of our dying soldiers, anticipating their wants, and soothing their last moments, with words and deeds, which woman's generous heart can only bestow.

The Brigade halted several hours a mile beyond the village, while large bodies of troops with General McClellan passed to the front. It was the first time that commander had been seen by the Brigade, and he was welcomed by enthusiastic cheers. Near this place we passed the smoking ruins of a covered bridge and a barn and shop, which had been burned a few hours previous by the enemy to hinder us from crossing the Catoctin Creek, and to destroy a quantity of grain which would have been useful to our army. The stream was however easily crossed a few yards below. A heavy cannonade was heard through the afternoon on the hills two miles in front, and now and then, squads of prisoners were marched to the rear, or wounded men came along alone, or supported by a comrade. At the Creek the columns divided, some taking the main road that led up through Turner's Pass, while others followed a narrow country road that diverged to the left, and led up the mountain to where the North Carolina forces under General D. H. Hill, were posted.

About five miles still further to the left, another turnpike led over the mountain at Crampton Pass, where Franklin's Corps was at this time advancing to that brilliant charge so memorable in the history of this campaign. General Duryée's Brigade at three o'clock, advanced up the turnpike for some distance, when turning to the right, along obscure roads and across fields, it came up to the mountain near our extreme right. The delays attending this advance had worn away the afternoon, and it was nearly sundown before the moment came for decisive action.

The Pennsylvania Reserves under General Meade, had been gallantly working their way up the mountain, and had nearly reached the summit, when their ammunition was expended. They were about to yield before the enemy who rallied with new vigor as the fortunes of battle seemed to threaten them. It was a critical moment, and Duryée's Brigade was just in time to strike a decisive blow. In a loud and cheerful voice the General ordered his men to advance, and they steadily pressed forward in perfect order, and with loud cheers, firing deadly volleys upon the enemy. In a few minutes they reached the crest of the mountain, and drove the foe in disorder down the further slope. It was now dark, and after learning with certainty that no hostile force was near, the Command bivouacked for the night on the field strewn with the rebel dead.* The total Union loss at South Mountain, was 328 killed, and 1463 wounded and missing. The loss of the enemy was estimated at 3000.

During the morning of the 15th, vast bodies of Union troops were concentrated along the road near the summit of the pass, and about 9 o'clock advanced down the National Road to Boonsboro, passing by the way a group of rebel hospital tents, near some barns that were filled with wounded. They belonged to Rode's Brigade of Alabama troops, (3d, 5th, 6th, 12th, and 26th regiments), which had opposed us in the battle of the previous evening, and formed a part of D. H. Hill's Division. Their Surgeon was first informed of the disaster that had befallen them, at ten o'clock on the evening previous, and was left with one man from each regiment, detailed as an attendant. Immense numbers of stragglers fell into our hands among the mountains, and the roadside was strewn with cast off knapsacks and the surplus clothing of the retreating enemy. A portion of the rear guard had been cut off a short time before by our cavalry, and were resting in a field near Boonsboro when we passed them. Here the road turned to the left towards Sharpsburgh, and along this we marched to within a mile of Keedysville, where the Brigade halted by the roadside, and remained from one o'clock till late in the evening.

While resting here, large bodies of troops, many of them full regiments just arrived from the north,

* See Appendix for Official Reports.

and as yet strangers to the hardships of the campaign, came up and passed. Some were singing the John Brown chorus, and others found occasion for merriment in commenting upon the picturesque appearance of our weathered and sun burnt soldiers. They all seemed cheerful, and as their long columns and full ranks marched by, their polished arms glistening in the sun, one could scarcely repress a sigh at the thought that with a certainty, hundreds of these men would fall in the battle, which all knew was now closely impending. Now and then a report of cannon was heard in the front, at no great distance. While in this spot we received intelligence that Harper's Ferry had been treacherously surrendered, with eleven thousand troops, seventy three cannon, and immense supplies, that would enable the enemy to throw their united forces across our way, and offer battle with numbers far greater than had ever yet been brought into action on the American continent.

At about eleven o'clock in the evening, Duryée's Brigade advanced through the village of Keedysville, and a little beyond turned by a narrow road to the right, crossed a new stone bridge and lay down for the night.

Every vehicle excepting cannon, caissons and ammunition wagons, had been stopped beyond the mountain by an imperative order of General McClellan, and in the morning we found ourselves again entirely destitute of food. From the general down to privates, the same equality prevailed, with this exception, that here and there a private, more provident than his comrades, and now taught the useful lesson of depending upon no transportation but his own, had saved a few crackers. The country around, was indeed the garden of Maryland, but it had recently been swept by over a hundred thousand rebels, and every article of food that had not been concealed by families was gone. Again we had recourse to the cornfields, but this staple article of food was too far ripened to be eaten without difficulty, and the greater part got no food, until a supply of "hard tack," sugar and coffee, came up in the afternoon.

An irregular cannonade continued through the day, and it was now apparent that no further advance would be made, except to meet the enemy in battle array. Several times in the afternoon, the bugle calls summoned the troops to arms, but the order to march did not come until about four o'clock, when the Divison of General Ricketts, marched along a narrow road, and across the Antietam at another stone bridge, directly towards the Potomac, and the right of the line of battle that was forming, some two miles distant. As the column came to the summit of a gentle swell, we observed that our line extended a mile or more in length, while other troops that had forded the Antietam below, were moving along in a parallel colums, some sixty or eighty yards to our left. The rear of these columns extended over behind the hills an unknown distance. Trains of artillery were also advancing by our side, and on a hill in front, the signal corps were engaged in transmitting their observations upon the position and movements of the enemy. The order of march was perfect, for just before moving, the regiments had been drawn up in hollow squares, and the most stringent orders against straggling or evading duty in battle were read.

Night began to close in, as the Brigade reached the edge of a cornfield, some forty rods beyond the dwelling of Mr. George Line. Here forming in column by division they marched through the cornfield, and wheeling to the left, as they reached the crest of a gentle swell of land, advanced with steady ranks directly towards the enemy, whose shells were bursting every moment in the air above them. By the time that the Brigade reached the edge of a piece of woods, about a quarter of a mile to the front, it was dark, and they laid down on their arms for the night, in line of battle, and only a few hundred yards from the enemy. Our Division was proceeded by that of the Pennsylvania Reserves under General Mead, who became slightly engaged before dark, with some loss. It is now known, that the enemy in front of our lines, on the right, consisted of Jackson's Division (Gen. J R. Jones commanding), on the west side of the Hagerstown turnpike, and partly in a piece of woods, and Ewell's Division, (Gen. Lawton commanding,) on his right, and directly opposite our front. The former of these Divisions comprised the Brigades of General's Winder, Jones, Taliafero, and Starke, and the latter those of General's Early, Hays, Trimble, and Lawton. Their batteries on this part of the field were those of Poague, Carpenter, Brockenborough, Raine, Caskie, and Wooding. The front lines were held by Winder's and Jones's Brigade west of the Turnpike, and by Lawton's and Trimble's to the east.

The night passed quietly away, with the exception of frequent firing on the picket lines of the opposing armies which were in close proximity At the first dawn of day on the memorable 17th, of September, skirmishing commenced in front and at sunrise, General Hooker, who now commanded the corps lately under McDowell, advanced his columns through the thin open woods, and opened the battle. The front lines were formed as on the preceding evening, and the artillery opened a vigorous fire as the infantry advanced, and from time to time took up new positions as the enemy retired.

The Division of General Doubleday, (late King's) formed on General Hooker's right, extending across, and to some distance beyond the Hagerstown turnpike. Seymour's Brigade of Meade's Division, on the left of Doubleday, engaged at an early hour in the morning, when having expended their ammunition they passed to the rear, and were relieved by Ricketts's Division. The enemy had advanced somewhat, as the Brigades of Generals Hartsuff and Duryée came up, the latter on the left, while the Brigade lately under Gen. Tower was held in the rear as a reserve. Thompson's and Matthew's batteries were brought up, and in a few moments the whole line was furiously engaged, and both parties with the most destructive effect. Duryée's Brigade having formed in columns by division and advanced across a plowed field, deployed into line as it came up to a cornfield, and held this position under a most destructive fire. For a time they drove the enemy before them, but heavy reënforcements were brought up, and they were in turn compelled to fall back, leaving long lines of dead across the field. An observer at this juncture counted eight or nine battle flags, as the steady ranks of the rebels advanced through the cornfield.

The Brigade as it fell back, rallied in a new position, partly sheltered by a few scraggy rocks, where by its enfilading fire, it prevented the enemy from carrying off the guns of Thompson's battery, which had been nearly silenced by the loss of many of its men in killed and wounded. This splendid artillery officer nobly sustained his reputation in the presence of the Brigade. His guns were held until heavy reënforcements came up under General Sumner, when the enemy were again forced to retire from the ground they had lately held, not in disorder, but slowly and in line, stubbornly contesting every yard of ground, with the greatest obstinacy.

The heroic Brigade of Gen. Duryée, when it was finally relieved, retired from the field with only fifteen or twenty men with their four colors. The number was increased soon after to nearly a hundred, and they lay the remainder of the day supporting batteries.

The effect of this encounter is thus described in Stonewall Jackson's official report of the battle.

"About sunrise, the Federal Infantry advanced in heavy force to the edge of the wood on the eastern side of the turnpike, driving in our skirmishers. Batteries were opened in front from the wood, with shell and canister, and our troops became exposed, for near an hour, to a terrific storm of shell, canister and musketry. General Jones having been compelled to leave the field, the command of Jackson's Division devolved upon General Starke. With heroic spirit, our lines advanced to the conflict, and maintained their position in the face of superior numbers, with stubborn resolution, sometimes driving the enemy before them, and sometimes compelled to fall back, before their well sustained and destructive fire. Fresh troops from time to time relieved the enemy's ranks, and the carnage on both sides was terrific. At an early hour General Starke was killed, Colonel Dougals (commanding Lawton's Brigade) was also killed. General Lawton Commanding Division, and Col. Walker Commanding Brigade were severely wounded. More than half of the Brigades of Lawton and Hays were either killed or wounded, and more than a third of Trimble's, and all the regimental Commanders in those Brigades except two were killed or wounded. Thinned in their ranks and exhausted of their ammunition, Jackson's Division and the Brigades of Lawton Hays and Trimble retired to the rear, and Hood of Longstreet's Command, again took the position from which he had been before relieved."

The battle continued with fearful violence through the day, and night closed in upon a scene of carnage that has few parallels in history. The Union armies had gained possession of the field with its sad trophies of blood, and all night long, and for days after, trains of ambulances were busy gathering up the wounded, and placing them in hospitals extemporized in the farm houses throughout the country in the rear.

On the night of the 18th, the enemy succeeded in crossing the Potomac at Shepardstown Ford, and our armies were allowed to rest. Supplies of every kind,—clothing, camp equipage and transportation had been lost or separated from the troops in the late campaign, and these must be restored before active aggressive movements could be made.

The army encamped for some miles along the Potomac, near the scene of the great battle, with the fresh graves of their companions in arms, and the trenches filled with unrecorded rebel dead in daily view. The wounded were gathered into hospitals and sent away from time to time, until only those with amputations or very severe injuries remained. These were collected into three great camp hospitals, until released by death, or so far recovered as to be able to return to their friends. Nothing was omitted which science or humanity could suggest, to alleviate their condition, yet the increasing number of fresh graves told from day to day how powerless were these agencies in staying the work of death. Yet in the hospitals, not less than on the field, did these worthy men evince heroic qualities, by painful sufferings bravely endured.

CHAPTER VII.

ENCAMPMENT ON THE POTOMAC. MARCH INTO VIRGINIA. BRIGADE REORGANIZED.

On the second day after the battle of Antietam, the Brigade advanced about a mile and a half, and bivouacked in a wood to the right of Sharpsburgh. On the 23d of September it removed to a point a mile above, and bivouacked in a wood near the river, adjacent to a canal landing known as New Industry, the head quarters being established at Mercersville, a hamlet half a mile above, and near the bank of the river.

A reorganization of Army Corps had been made pending the movements in Maryland, and although dating on the 12th of September, the arrangement did not become generally known until after the battles. The 1st and 2d Corps of the late army of Virginia, became the 11th and 12th Corps, and the 3d Corps (late McDowell's) became known as the 1st Corps. Gen. Hooker having been wounded, the command of the 1st Corps was assigned to Major General Reynolds. So far as the new 1st Corps was concerned, this was simply restoring the old number, which the greater portion of these troops had received when the Corps were first organized on the 13th of March previous. It had originally included the Divisions of McDowell,

Franklin and McCall. The second of these became the 6th Corps on the 22d of July; General King succeeded McDowell; the 2d Division under Ord, and afterwards Ricketts, was formed of new troops, and McCall was succeeded by Reynolds and Meade

On the 6th of October, the Commander in Chief telegraphed to Gen. McClellan, by order of the President, directing him to cross the Potomac, and give battle to the enemy or drive him south, as the roads were then in good condition. The President advised that the interior line between the enemy and Washington should be taken, rather than that up the Shenandoah Valley But delays attributed to insufficiency of supplies and other causes, occurred until the 26th of October. The Brigade of Gen. Duryée, after remaining in bivouack in the woods on the Potomac, until the 11th of October, received supplies of tents and clothing, and encamped on a ridge in the open fields, about half a mile from their former site, and overlooking the battle field.

The duties of the Brigade were chiefly limited to picketing the line of the canal, about 3 miles. The river channel was fordable in several places in this distance, but no hostilities occurred along this line.

On the 3d of October, General Duryée received leave of absence for thirty days, and did not rejoin the Brigade until on the eve of the changes which broke up the old associations, and introduced new ones at Bealton, in November following.

The command, devolved upon Col. T. F McCoy of the 107th Penn'a, the senior Colonel then present, and he continued in this position until relieved by Gen. Nelson Taylor early in November.

During the encampment on the Potomac, few events occurred to diversify camp life. The raid of Stuart into Pennsylvania, on the 10th of October, led to prompt action among the troops, to meet and check the enemy should he attempt to recross in that vicinity, sections of artillery supported by infantry were posted in the roads, and the guards were strongly reënforced, especially at points where it could be forded, but this vigilance availed little, and was soon ended by the report that the rebels had recrossed the Potomac many miles below.

The beautiful autumnal weather which had thus far prevailed, since the troops had held their position, began to show indications of the approach of winter before marching orders were received. The 26th of October opened bleak and dreary, but late in the forenoon, orders were recieved to pack up and march in the midst of a cold dismal rain. The storm continued through the day and night, as the Brigade left the now familiar scenes of Antietam, and wound its way through Sharpsburgh, and over the Elk Ridge range of hills into Pleasant Valley.

The darkness became intense, the roads were encumbered with trains, and our advance was tedious and finally came to an end, the regiments still standing in the road. As if resolved to be happy in spite of misery, a glee club in the 104th Regiment here extemporized a concert, and there is scarcely a piece of familiar vocal comic, sentimental or patriotic music, that was not executed by these amateurs. Gradually, the men gathered around fires built of the fences along the road side, and wore away the night as best they were able.

The next day cleared off cold and windy, and the Brigade encamped late in the afternoon near Birkettsville, at the foot of Crampton Pass. The churches and school houses of the village were still used as hospitals, and the cemetery with its long rows of new graves, showed that the work of death had not ceased with the roar of battle. Many of the inmates of these hospitals were our late enemies, yet they received attentions exactly similar to our own men, and notices were posted on the doors, strictly forbidding visitors from makng presents of articles of luxury or comfort, *exclusively to those of either party.*

On the 30th the command crossed the Potomac at Berlin on a pontoon bridge of sixty-two boats, and on the 7th of November, came out from behind the Bull Run mountains at Warrenton.

The details of this march may be briefly stated. The route led through Lovettsville, Waterford, Hamilton, and along the turnpike to near Snicker's Gap, when it turned to the left, and followed the east side of the Blue Ridge through Bloomfield, and crossed the Manassas Gap rail road, two miles east of Rectortown. The trains were guarded each day by a regiment of infantry, and reports of cannon were daily heard in front, as our cavalry and artillery that led the advance skirmished with the rear guard of the retiring enemy. The result of these encounters was unknown to us, except as learned from newspapers, yet they served to keep up an interest in the march and led to the expectation of daily meeting the enemy at bay. The command halted on the night of the 5th, on the estate of Colonel R. M. Dulaney of the 6th Virginia Cavalry, whose position in the rebel service, exposed his property to unusual waste.

This might not have occurred had it not been ascertained that he had concealed in his barns a large quantity of salt and several barrels of powder, apparently for aid and comfort to the enemy These were effectually scattered, and quantities of grain, potatoes and bacon were appropriated by the troops.

These irregularities are recorded as an exception to the usual custom of our troops, who seldom took liberties with private property with the design to waste.

If they burnt fences, it was to preserve comfort and health, and there have been occasions when they would have been without food, had they not taken that which the country around them afforded.

These occurrences were exceptional, and in no case due to neglect on the part of officers charged with the duty of furnishing supplies. The casualties and necessities of the service in the best ordered armies, will occasionally find the troops in want.

Upon crossing into Virginia, General Ricketts was relieved at his own request, and assigned to the command of the defences of Harper's Ferry, and General John Gibbon, holding the rank of Brigadier of Volunteers, and that of Captain in the 4th U S. Artillery, was placed in command of the Division. He had for several months commanded a Brigade in the first Division of the same Corps. At Warrenton, our troops were reviewed for the last time by Major General McClellan, on the 10th of November, and he was succeeded by Major General Burnside. This change of leaders, involved a modification of plans, and in the delays which followed, the enemy succeeded in withdrawing the forces which had been left behind us in the Shenandoah Valley, and in massing heavy bodies of troops in our front.

The First Division of the First Corps under General Doubleday, marched from Warrenton to the Rappahannock rail road crossing on the 8th of November, and arrived in time to save the bridge from destruction. The enemy had during the absence of our armies in Maryland, restored communication with the north bank of the Rappahannock, and at this time, a train of cars might have been run from Washington to Richmond, but for the military reasons that prevented.

On the 11th, the remainder of the Corps marched to Bealton Station, and arriving at a late hour in the evening, groped their way out into the fields adjacent, and bivouacked for the night. It was intensely dark, and the camp was formed with that disordered arrangement, that may be always expected when troops weary from a long march, halt at night on ground, with which none of them are familiar.

On the 13th General Duryée returned to the Brigade, but only to find an officer who was his junior in commission, in command of the Division, to which by the usages of the service he should have been assigned. The General immediately represented his claims before General Burnside, who although favorably inclined, deemed it proper to refer back the matter to the Corps Commander (Gen.

Reynolds,) as coming more directly within his province to decide. The latter from reasons not within our knowledge, saw fit to defer the matter for the present, as the army was on the march, and Gen. Duryée received leave of absence to return to Washington. He drew up the Brigade on a new site, caused a camp to be laid out with the nicest care, and taking leave of the officers and men, as was then hoped but for a little season, left them, never to return as their commander. There was a feeling prevalent among the officers of the Brigade, that great injustice was done to Gen. Duryée in not appointing him to the command of the Division.

On the 14th, the Division was reviewed by General Gibbon, and on the evening of that day, he caused a letter to be read to the officers of the First Brigade, in which from observations made in a camp laid out at midnight, and from appearances due to recent service, he saw fit to draw conclusions deemed by every one unjust and insulting. This was followed on the 16th, by a reorganization of the Division, which broke up many pleasant associations, and changed the relative seniority of regimental commanders, from that which they would have otherwise enjoyed. These grievances were, it is believed, limited chiefly to the officers, as the men knew little of the offensive letter, and felt still less, the bitterness which it occasioned. The unwelcome relations lasted but a few days, and the battle of Fredericksburgh, brought relief, by giving a new Division commander. We will now briefly notice the changes that were made.

During the Maryland campaign, the 16th Maine regiment (3 years), was added to the 3d, and the 136th Pennsylvania (9 months), to the 2d Brigade. The organization of the 1st Division 1st Corps before and after November 16th, was as follows:

BEFORE THE CHANGE:

1st *Brigade*, 97th N. Y.; 104th N Y; 105th N. Y.; 107th Pa.

2d *Brigade*, 26th N Y; 94th N Y; 88th Pa.; 90th Pa.; 136th Pa.

3d *Brigade*, 83d N. Y.; (9th N Y S. M.); 11th Pa.; 12th Mass.; 13th Mass.; 16th Me.

AFTER THE CHANGE:

1st *Brigade*, 94th N Y; 104th N Y.; 105th N Y; 107th Pa.; 16th Me.

2d *Brigade*, 26th N Y; 90th Pa.; 136th Pa.; 12th Mass.

3d *Brigade*, 83d N Y; (9th N Y S M.); 97th N Y; 11th Pa.; 88th Pa.; 13th Mass.

The commanders of Brigades became as follows:

1st *Brigade*, Col. Adrian R. Root, of the 94th N Y Vols.

2d *Brigade*, Col. Lyle, of the 90th Pa. Vols.

3d *Brigade*, Brigadier General Nelson Taylor, formerly Colonel of the 72d N Y Vols. It is due to these officers to record, that they were all capable and efficient, and that they enjoyed the confidence of their commands.

General Duryée did not again resume command in the field, and on the 5th of January 1863, resigned his commission as Brigadier General of Volunteers. Returning to private life, he carried with him the affectionate regard of the Brigade he had led during seven months, and through seven battles. Yet he left behind a memory and example not soon to be forgotten, and whatever fortunes may await his old companions in arms, in their career of honorable service, they will look back with pleasure and pride, to the time when they served in the Heroic Brigade.

APPENDIX.

LIST OF OFFICERS ON THE BRIGADE STAFF, AND IN THE SEVERAL REGIMENTS COMPOSING THE BRIGADE COMMANDED BY GEN. DURYEE IN 1862.

BRIGADE STAFF.

Assistant Adjutant-General, Capt. William B. C. Duryée; wounded at Antietam.

Brigade Commissary, Capt. Edwin D. Willard, (U. S. V.)

Brigade Quartermasters, Lieut. Henry V Colt (104 N. Y V.); served till the last of June, 1862 Capt. Wm. H. H. Crandall (107th Pa. V), promoted to Asst. Quartermaster, U. S. V

Brigade Surgeon, J Theodore Heard, (U. S. V.).

Aids, Lieutenants J. De Lany (101 N Y V) Charles A. Kenney (104 N. Y V.)

NINETY SEVENTH REGIMENT, NEW YORK VOLUNTEERS.

FIELD AND STAFF.

Colonel, Charles Wheelock, Jan. 16, 1862.
Lieut. Col, John Pembroke Spofford, Oct. 20, 1861.
Major, Charles Northup, Dec. 16, 1861.
Surgeons, Nelson D. Ferguson, Oct. 8, 1861; transferred to 8th N. Y Cavalry.
Langdon I. Marvin, March 8, 1862; resigned June 15, 1862.
Franklin B. Hough, July 3, 1862.

Assistant Surgeons, Aaron Cornish. Oct. 23, 1861 ;
dismissed Sept. 8, 1862.
Nelson Isham, Sept. 25, 1862.
George S. Little, Oct, 13, 1862.
Adjutants, Charles Buck, Sept. 30, 1861 ; resigned
March 25, 1862.
George D. Foster, Jr., March 25, 1862 ;
resigned Sept. 10, 1862.
Dennis J. Downing, Nov. 1, 1862; Subsequently Captain of Co., H. He was taken prisoner at Bull Run, lost a leg at Gettysburgh, and is now Captain in the Veteran Reserve Corps.
Quartermasters, Joel T. Comstock, Dec. 31, 1861:
resigned Sept. 12, 1862.
Lewis H. Rowan, Sept. 12, 1862.
Chaplain, John V Ferguson, (Meth Ep.) Nov. 11, 1861.

LINE OFFICERS.

Captains.

A. Samuel M. Ferguson, Sept. 30, 1861; discharged.
Chester D. Fenton, Oct. 4, 1862; declined.
Alexander L. Jillson, Oct. 4, 1862.
B. Aaron Dayan Parsons, Sept. 30, 1861.
C. Stephen Manchester, Sept. 30, 1861; discharged for disability.
Andrew Wood, Sept. 12, 1862.
D. Rouse S. Egelston, Oct. 16th, 1861.
E. Richard Jones, Oct. 15th, 1861; mortally wounded at Bull Run.
F. Stephen G. Hutchinson, Oct 16th, 1861; discharged.

E. Gerry Spencer, Sept. 22, 1862; declined.
Delos E. Hall, Sept. 22, 1862.
G. William Smith, Oct. 16, 1861; discharged Oct. 31 1862.
H. Antoine Brendle, Oct. 16, 1861; discharged.
William A. Hopkins, Sept. 25, 1862.
I. James P Leslie, Oct. 15, 1861; resigned.
Romeyn Roof, July 15, 1862; taken prisoner at Bull Run, Aug. 30, 1862; did not rejoin the regiment; resigned.
K. Gustavus M. Palmer, Dec. 13, 1861; wounded at Fredericksburgh, and is now serving in the Veteran Reserve Corps.

First Lieutenants.

A. Elmer E. Sawyer, Sept. 30, 1861.
B. William R. Parsons, Sept. 30, 1861.
C. Lewis H. Rowan, Sept. 30, 1861; app. Qr. Mr.
Thomas Watters, Sept. 12, 1862.
D. Dwight S. Faville, Oct. 16, 1861; killed Aug. 30, 1862, at Bull Run.
Isaac Hall, Aug. 30, 1862.
E. Maross Jenkins, Oct. 15, 1861; dismissed by court martial, G. O. 166.
Justus O. Rockwell, Oct. 24, 1862.
F. E. Gerry Spencer, Oct. 16, 1861; promoted to Captain.
Delos E. Hall, Sept. 22, 1862; promoted to Captain.
G. Francis Murphy, Oct. 16, 1861; wounded and taken prisoner at Bull Run; left on the field and taken to Washington; again taken prisoner at Gettysburgh, and many months in a Richmond prison.

H. Edward Thomas, Oct. 16, 1861; resigned.
    Francis T. Brennan, Nov. 19, 1862; Acting Adjutant at Antietam, where he was wounded. He was killed in the battles of the Wilderness, June 1864. Few officers were more brave or patriotic.

I. Romeyn Roof, Oct 15, 1861; promoted to Captain.
    William A. Hopkins, July 15, 1862; promoted Captain of Co. H.

K. Joseph Warren, Dec. 13, 1861; discharged.
    Rush P Cady, Sept. 24, 1862; mortally wounded at Gettysburgh.

Second Lieutenants.

A. Charles D .Fenton, Dec. 16, 1861; taken prisoner at Bull Run, Aug. 30, 1862; did not rejoin the regiment; resigned.
    Alexander L. Jillson, Oct. 4, 1862; promoted to Captain.
    William J Morrin, Nov. 6, 1862; (killed at Gettysburgh.)

B. Dennis J. Downing, Dec. 21, 1861; promoted to Adjutant.
    Adelbert Jones, Nov. 1, 1862.

C. Andrew Wood, Dec. 17, 1861; promoted to Captain.

D. Isaac Hall, Jan. 15, 1862; promoted to 1st. Lieutenant.
    James H. Styles, Aug. 30, 1862; (killed at Gettysburgh).

E. Justus O. Rockwell, Dec. 19, 1861; promoted to 1st. Lieutenant.
    Joseph H. Smith, Oct. 24, 1862.

F. George W Skinner, Jan. 13, 1862; resigned.
   Jacob W Carner, April 25. 1862; discharged Nov. 3, 1862.
G. John T. Norton, Dec. 21 1861.
H. Louis Dallarmi, Dec. 17, 1861; killed at Antietam, September 17, 1862.
I. Lewis H. Carpenter, Feb. 14, 1862.
K. Rush P Cady, Feb. 18, 1862; promoted to 1st Lieutenant.
   George Alexander, Sept. 24, 1862.

ONE HUNDRED AND FOURTH REGIMENT, NEW YORK VOLUNTEERS.

FIELD AND STAFF.

Colonels, John Rorbach, March 15, 1861; discharged.
   Lewis C. Skinner, Oct. 21, 1862; declined.
   Gilbert G. Prey, Oct. 21, 1862.
Lieut. Colonels, R. Wells Kenyon, March 8 1861; discharged.
   Lewis C. Skinner, Sept. 11, 1862; promoted to Colonel.
   Gilbert G. Prey, Oct. 21, 1862; promoted to Colonel.
   Henry G. Tuthill, Oct. 21, 1862.
Majors, Lewis C. Skinner, March 15, 1862; promoted to Lieut. Colonel.
   Gilbert G. Prey, Sept. 11, 1862; promoted to Lieut. Colonel.
   John R. Strang, Oct. 21, 1862.
Surgeon, Enos G. Chase, Nov. 29, 1861.
Assistant Surgeons, Douglass S. Langdon, Dec. 10, 1861; resigned.
   Charles H. Richmond, Aug. 8, 1862.

Chaplains, Daniel Russell (F W Bap.), Aug. 18, 1862; resigned.
Ferdinand DeW Ward, (O. S. Presb.)
Adjutants, Frederick T. Vance, March 15, 1862; resigned.
George L. Snyder, Aug. 31, 1862.
Quartermaster, Henry V Colt, Jan. 11, 1862.

LINE OFFICERS.

Captains.

A. Henry G. Tuthill, Sept. 30, 1861; promoted to Major.
Albert S. Haver, Oct. 21, 1862.
B. Lehman H. Day, Oct. 18, 1861; resigned.
Henry A. Wiley, April 8, 1862.
C. Stephen L. Wing, Oct. 9, 1861; discharged.
Nelson J. Wing, Oct. 8, 1862.
D. Zophar Simpson, Oct. 18, 1861; discharged.
George H. Starr, Sept. 12, 1862.
E. Hugh C. Lattimore, Oct. 23, 1861; discharged.
Benjamin F Spencer, Sept. 12, 1862.
F. Gilbert G. Prey, Dec. 5, 1861; promoted to Major.
Luman F Dow, Sept. 11, 1862.
G. James A. Gault, Nov. 14, 1861.
H. James K. Selleck, Dec. 12, 1861.
I. John Kelly, Dec. 12, 1861; killed at battle of Antietam.
Charles W Fisher, Sept. 17, 1862.
K. John C. Thompson, Dec. 12, 1861; dismissed.
William C. Wilson, July 28, 1862.

First Lieutenants.

A. Lewis C. Skinner, Sept. 30, 1861; promoted to Major.

ONE HUNDRED AND FOURTH REGIMENT, N. Y. V

A. Alexander S. Haver, March 15, 1862; promoted to Captain.
   Reuben R. Weed, Oct. 21, 1862.
B. Henry A. Wiley, Oct. 18, 1861; promoted to Captain.
   Homer Stull, April 8 1862.
C. Henry Runyon, Oct. 9, 1861; discharged.
   Nelson J. Wing, Sept. 17. 1862; promoted to Captain.
   Alfred P Van Dresser, Oct. 8, 1862.
D. Jacob H. Stull, Jan. 4, 1862; resigned.
   Thomas Johnston, Oct. 31, 1862.
E. William P Lozier, Oct. 23, 1861; discharged.
   William L. Trembly, Sept. 18, 1862.
F. Luman F Dow, Dec. 5, 1861; promoted to Captain.
   Austin N Richardson, Sept. 11, 1862.
G. John P Rudd, Nov. 2, 1861; killed in action.
   John R. Strang, Sept. 12, 1862; promoted to Major.
   Adam Dixon, Oct. 21, 1862.
H. Ephraim B. Wheeler, Dec, 12, 1861; resigned.
I. John J. McCaffrey, Jan. 9, 1862; died.
   John Daly, Sept. 17, 1862.
K. John H. Miller, Jan. 7, 1862; ——
   William C. Wilson July 19, 1862; promoted to Captain.
   Charles A. Kenney, July 28, 1862.

Second Lieutenants.

Albert S. Haver, Nov. 12, 1861; promoted to 1st Lieutenant.
Robert J. Rogers, March 18, 1862; declined.

A. Reuben R. Weed, April 14, 1862; promoted to 1st Lieutenant.
Albert T. Lamson, Oct. 21, 1862.
B. Homer Stull, Jan. 4, 1862; promoted to 1st Lieutenant.
William J. Starks, April 8, 1862.
C. Nelson J Wing, Nov. 11, 1861; promoted to 1st Lieutenant.
Andrew J Andrews, Sept. 17, 1862.
D. George V Starr, March 6, 1862; promoted to Captain.
Edward A. Tuthill, Sept. 12, 1862.
E. William L. Trembly, Jan. 18, 1862; promoted to 1st Lieutenant.
Adoniram J. Rose, Sept. 18, 1862.
F. W J. Heustreet, Nov. 14, 1861; resigned.
Austin M. Richardson, June 28, 1862; promoted to 1st Lieutenant.
John McDonnell, Sept. 11, 1862.
G. John R. Strang, March 6, 1862; promoted to 1st Lieutenant.
Adam Dixon, Sept. 12, 1862; promoted to 1st Lieutenant.
Walter S. Stephens, Oct. 21, 1862.
H. Thomas Johnston, March 4, 1862; promoted to 1st Lieutenant Co. D.
James W Dow, Oct. 31, 1862.
I. Charles W Fisher, Jan. 9, 1862; promoted to Captain.
James H. Cain, Sept. 17, 1862.
Wm. C. Wilson, Dec. 12, 1861; promoted to 1st Lieutenant.

K. Charles A. Kenny, July 17, 1862; promoted to 1st Lieutenant.
John B. Meserve, July 28, 1862.

ONE HUNDRED AND FIFTH REGIMENT N. Y VOLUNTEERS

FIELD AND STAFF.

Colonels, James M. Fuller, March 26, 1862; resigned.
  Howard Carroll, Aug. 2, 1862; mortally wounded at Antietam.
  John W Shedd, Oct. 6, 1862; mustered out March 17, 1863.
Lieut. Colonels, Homer Achilles, Jan. 6, 1862.
  Howard Carroll, March 27, 1862; promoted to Colonel.
  Richard Whiteside, Oct. 6, 1862; mustered out March 17, 1863.
Majors, John W Shedd, March 26, 1862; promoted to Colonel.
  Daniel A. Sharpe, Oct. 6, 1862; March 17, 1863.
Surgeons, David C, Chamberlin, Oct. 28, 1861.
Assist. Surgeons, James W Casey, March 24, 1862; mustered out March, 17, 1863.
  John T. Brown, Sept. 17, 1862.
Chaplains, Byron P Russell, (F W. Bap.) March 15, 1862.
Adjutants, Daniel A. Sharpe, Nov 27, 1862; promoted to Major.
  John J. White. Oct. 6, 1862; mustered out March 17, 1863.
Quartermasters, Charles Strong, March 26, 1862; resigned.
  Jerome J. Shedd, Aug. 12, 1862.

Captains.

A. Richard Whiteside, Nov. 16, 1861; promoted to Lieut. Col.
John C. Whiteside, Oct. 6, 1862.
B. James B. N. De Long, Nov. 26, 1861; discharged.
Charles F Rudger, Sept. 30, 1862.
C. Henry E. Smith, Nov. 30, 1861; resigned.
Thomas A. Steadman, Oct. 13, 1862; mustered out March 17, 1863.
D. Isaac S. Tichenor, March 18, 1862; mustered out March 17, 1863.
E. George Babcock, Dec. 26, 1862; discharged.
Willis Benham, Oct. 6, 1862; mustered out March 17, 1863.
F. Abraham Moore, Jan. 6, 1862; mustered out March 17, 1863.
G. John McMahon, March 25, 1862.
H. Patrick W Bradley, March 25, 1862; mustered out, March 17, 1863.
I. Thomas Purcell, March 25, 1862; resigned.
Joseph E. Conway, Sept. 22, 1862.
K. Salah J. Wilbur, Feb. 18, 1862.

First Lieutenants.

A. John Whiteside, Nov. 16, 1861; promoted to Captain.
Benjamin Whiteside, Oct. 6, 1862.
B. Charles F Rudgers, Nov. 26, 1861; promoted to Captain.
Frederick J. Massey, Sept. 30, 1862.
C. Thomas A. Steadman, Nov. 30, 1861; promoted to Captain.
John De Graff, Oct. 13, 1862.

ONE HUNDRED AND FIFTH REGIMENT, N. Y. V 141

D. Horace D. Bennett, Dec 11, 1861; dismissed.
  Augustus Field. Oct. 17, 1862.
E. Willis Benham, Dec. 26, 1861; promoted to
  Captain.
  Lucius F Rolfe, Oct. 6, 1862.
F William Clark, Jan. 6, 1862; discharged.
  William Knowles, Sept. 12, 1862; mustered
  out, March 17, 1863.
G. Dennis Graham, March 25, 1862; discharged.
  Isaac Doolittle, Oct. 9, 1862.
H. David C Smith, March 25, 1862; discharged.
I. Michael McMullen, March 25, 1862; mustered
  out, March 17, 1863.
K. David Gould Jr., Feb. 18, 1862; resigned.
  Eli D. Woodworth, July 10, 1862; mustered
  out, March 17, 1863.

Second Lieutenants.

A. George M. Dickey, Jan. 5, 1862; resigned.
  Thomas Burrows, Sept. 10, 1862.
B. Frederick J. Massey, Feb. 6, 1862; promoted
  to 1st Lieut.
  Charles F Mesler, Sept. 30, 1862.
C. John De Graff, March 20, 1862; promoted to
  1st Lieut.
  George T. Bushnell, Oct. 13, 1862; mustered
  out, March 17, 1863.
D. Augustus Field, March 22, 1862; promoted to
  1st Lieut.
  Oscar Hawkins, Oct. 17, 1862.
E. John I. White, March 11, 1862; promoted to
  Adjutant.

Lucius F Rolfe, Oct. 6, 1862; mustered out, March 17, 1863.
F. William Knowles, Feb. 20, 1862; promoted to 1st Lieut.
Edwin A. Dayton, Sept. 12, 1862.
G. Isaac Doolittle, March 25, 1862; promoted to 1st Lieut.
George W Connolly, Oct. 9, 1862; promoted to 1st Lieut. Co. H.
H. Joseph E. Conway, March 25, 1862; promoted to Captain; mustered out as 2d Lieut. March 17, 1863.
George French, Sept. 22, 1862.
I. Charles E. Buckley, March 25, 1862; killed in action.
Garvin Longmuir, Sept. 17, 1862.
K. Eli D. Woodworth, March 27, 1862; resigned.
George Wilber, July 10, 1862; mustered out, March 17, 1863.

ONE HUNDRED AND SEVENTH, PENN'A VOLS

FIELD AND STAFF.

Colonels, Thomas A. Ziegle, August 15, 1861; died July 16, 1862.
Thomas F McCoy, August 5, 1862.
Lieut. Colonel, Robert W McAllen, Nov 7, 1861; resigned Dec. 20, 1862.
Majors, Jacob Forney, Dec. 1, 1861; died Oct. 16, 1862.
James MacThompson, Oct. 17, 1862.
Surgeons, John G. Frow, March 7, 1862; resigned Aug. 1, 1862.
James F Hutchinson, Aug. 15, 1862.

Assist. Surgeons, James F Hutchinson. March 7,
1861 : promoted to Surgeon.
H. G. Warrall Jr., Aug. 18, 1862;
promoted to Surgeon. 173 Pa.
Nov 14, 1862.
Edwin R. Wescott, Aug. 4. 1862.
R. S. Dana. Sept. 12. 1862.

Adjutants, Henry M. House, Nov. 28. 1861.

Quartermasters, Wm. H. H. Crandall, Dec. 10,
1861; promoted to Brigade
Q. M.
Samuel Lyon, July, 19, 1862.

Chaplains, Wm. T. Campbell, (Prot. Episc.) March
14, 1862.

LINE OFFICERS.

Captains.

A. Jacob Dorsheimer, Sept. 28, 1861.
B. James Mac Thompson, Oct. 5, 1861; promoted
to Major.
C. James Deegan, Oct. 12, 1861; resigned Oct.
21, 1862.
Thomas A. Deegan, Nov. 5, 1862.
D. John A. Moore, Dec. 10, 1861.
E. Emanuel D. Roath, Oct 10, 1861.
F. Elias W H. Eisenbeise, Jan. 22, 1862.
G. Morris Murphy, Oct. 11, 1861; resigned, June
30, 1862.
Edwin E. Zeigle, Aug. 30, 1862.
H. John T. Dick, Nov. 5, 1861; killed, Aug. 30,
1862.
George W Z. Black, Aug. 30, 1862.

I. Henry J. Shaeffer, Dec. 27, 1861.
K. A. Jackson Brand, Oct. 8, 1861.

First Lieutenants.

A. Thomas R. Scheffer, Feb. 1, 1862.
B. Thomas H. N. McPherson, Oct. 5, 1861.
C. James Corcoran, Nov. 28, 1861.
D. A. Wilson Norris, Nov 20, 1861.
E. James A. Carman, Nov 1, 1861.
F. Oscar Templeton, Jan. 1, 1862.
G. Hiram Chance, Feb. 14, 1862; resigned, Sept. 15, 1862.
James B. Thomas, Sept. 15, 1862.
H. Samuel Lyon, Nov 21, 1861; promoted to Q. M.
I. Wm. H. Bowman, Jan. 13, 1862; resigned, May 23, 1862.
Wm. N Black, May, 30, 1862.
K. Benj. Rodes, Oct. 8, 1861.

Second Lieutenants.

A. Oliver P Stair, Jan. 1, 1862.
B. William Graeff, Oct. 8, 1861; resigned, June 6, 1862.
Jacob V Gish, July 29, 1862.
C. Jeremiah Deegan, Nov. 28, 1861.
D. James N. Sterrett, Jan. 16, 1862; discharged Sept. 20, 1862.
E. John F Williams, Oct. 24, 1862.
F. Wm. H. Scott, Oct. 1, 1862; resigned, Aug. 12, 1862.
G. Edwin E. Zeigle, Feb. 22, 1862; promoted to Captain.
H. Geo. W Z. Black, Oct. 5, 1861.
I. David S. Matthews, Jan. 13, 1862.
K. Benj. Cook, Oct. 8, 1861.

ORGANIZATION OF THE SEVERAL REGIMENTS.

THE 97TH REGIMENT N Y VOLS. was organized at Boonville under an authorization dated September 13, 1861, and while forming were known as the Conklin Rifles. The companies were mainly raised as follows: Companies A and C, in Boonville, B in Lewis Co., D and F in Salisbury, E in Prospect and vicinity, G in Herkimer Co., H in Utica and Lowville, I in Little Falls, and K in Rome. It was mustered into service at Boonville, Feb. 18, 1862, left Boonville March 12th, received its arms at New York, and arrived in Washington on the 20th of March. After a brief sojourn on Kalorama Heights, it was ordered to garrison Fort Corcoran, and the works adjacent, until the formation of Duryée's Brigade, when it was ordered to Cloud's Mills, and became identified with that organization.

In the fall of 1863, it received large accessions from conscripts and substitutes, and early in 1864 nearly a hundred and fifty of its men reënlisted. The regiment suffered heavily at Gettysburgh, and more recently in the campaign under Gen. Grant.

THE 104TH REGIMENT N. Y VOLS. was formed by the consolidation of the Wadsworth Guards of seven companies, raised at Geneseo, and the Morgan Guards of three companies, raised at Troy. The depot at Geneseo, was authorized on the 24th of Sept., 1861, at first under Gen. Jas. Wood, Jr., but he soon resigned, and was succeeded by Col. John Rorbach, who completed the organization, and became its first Colonel. Henry V. Colt of

146 ORGANIZATION OF THE 105TH N. Y. V

Geneseo, was appointed Acting Quartermaster and Acting Adjutant. Barracks for the regiment were erected near the village of Geneseo, where it remained until February, 1862, when over 700 men who had been recruited there were removed to Albany.

The organization was completed on the 7th of March, and on the 22d of that month left the state, after first receiving their arms and camp equipage at the city of New York. The companies were mustered into the service on the following dates; A on the 30th of September; B on the 7th; C on the 9th; D on the 18th, and E on the 23d of October; F on the 5th of December; G on the 14th of November, 1861, and H, I, and K, on the 8th of March, 1862. On leaving the state, the strength of the Command was 971 officers and men.

THE 105TH REGIMENT N. Y VOLS. was organized in special camps at Le Roy and Rochester, and was formed by a consolidation of two thin regiments. Company A was raised in Wyoming and Genesee Co., B in Niagara, C in Monroe and Orleans, D in Niagara and Cattaraugus, E in Genesee and Wyoming, F in Orleans and Monroe, G, H, and I, in Rochester, and K in Cattaraugus. The three Rochester companies were at first intended for an Irish Brigade.

The regiment left Le Roy, March 31st, 1862, and arrived the next day at New York; received there their arms and equipage. On the 6th proceeded to Washington by way of Elizabethport, Easton, and Harrisburgh, and arrived on the morning of the 6th. After remaining at the Seventh Street

Barracks until the 15th they joined Duryée's Brigade at Cloud's Mills, Va., and subsequently shared its fortunes. The regiment lost 120 at Bull Run, in killed, wounded and prisoners. At South Mountain, their loss was 2 killed and 12 wounded, and at Antietam they lost in killed and wounded 89 officers and men. During the year 1862, they had 49 men killed in battle and lost 2 officers and 39 men from wounds, and other causes.

Col. Fuller, the first Colonel, left at Cedar Mountain a few days after the battle, and Lieut. Col. Carroll who succeeded to the command, led the regiment until mortally wounded at Antietam. Capt. Whiteside then assumed command, until succeeded by Major Sharpe, Oct. 26. Col. Shedd returned about Dec. 18th.

The 105th regiment was consolidated with the 94th N. Y V., March 17, 1863, near Belle Plain, Va. Each of the two regiments were first reduced to five equalized companies, the letters A to E, being assigned to the 94th, and those from F to K, to the 105th. The 94th retained its number, Colonel, Lieut. Col., Major, Chaplain, Adjutant, one Assistant Surgeon, and five sets of line officers, the remaining officers and the N. C. Staff being taken from the 105th. The following officers of the 105th, were rendered supernumerary by this consolidation, and were honorably discharged. Col. J. W Shedd, Lieut. Col. R. Whiteside, Maj. D. A. Sharpe, Adj. J. W White, Assist. Surg. J. W Casey; Captains A. Moore, I. S. Tichenor, W Benham, T. A. Stedman, and P W Bradley; 1st Lieuts. M. McMullen, W Knowles, and E. D.

Woodworth, and 2d Lieuts. L. F Rolfe, G. W Connolly, J E. Conway, J. H. Bushnell, and G. Wilbur.

Companies E and F, became F; G and H, G; A and I, H; B and C, I; and D and K, K.

THE 107TH REGIMENT, PENN'A VOLS. was formed by the consolidation of the 107th and 108th regiments March 7, 1862. The former was recruited in Sullivan, Luzerne, Schuylkill, York, Lebanon, Dauphin, Mifflin, Cumberland, Perry, and Lancaster Counties, and was assembled at Chambersburgh. The latter was raised in Bedford, Franklin, Cumberland, Fulton, and Perry Counties, by Colonel Robert W McAllen, and was assembled at Harrisburgh, where they were consolidated. The 107th retained its number and Colonel, while the Colonel of the 108th came in as Lieutenant Colonel. It was organized and mustered into the service at Harrisburgh by Capt. R. O. Dodge, March 8, 1862. It then numbered 34 officers, and 863 enlisted men. It left Harrisburgh March 9, 1862, reached Washington the next day, and on the 2d of April was ordered to Upton's Hill, to garrison forts. It joined Duryée's Brigade on the 16th of April, and is still in the service, a large portion of the regiment having reënlisted.

CASUALTIES IN BATTLE.

In the absence of records, we are able to present complete lists of casualties in two regiments only. Early and repeated efforts were made to obtain from the officers of each an authentic list, but from the failure of the mails or other causes, only partial returns have been received. This statement is made with regret, and as an apology for the manifest imperfection of the following lists.

KILLED AND WOUNDED IN ACTION IN THE 97TH REGIMENT, N. Y. V.

At Rappahannock Station, Aug. 23, John Schneider, private in Co. H, lost an arm, and Sergt. J. W Smith, Co. E, was bruised in side.

At Bull Run, Aug. 30, the regiment lost 7 in killed, 42 wounded, and 61 missing, mostly prisoners. Of the former, we have at hand only the names of, 1st Lieut. Dwight Faville, Co. D; privates Bartholomew Stuber, Philip Schumacker, and John Wormuth, of Co. H, and James Bruce of Co. K. Of the wounded, we have only the names of Capt. Richard Jones, Co. E; 1st Lieut. Francis Murphy, Co. G; private Benj. Miller, Co. B; private Wm. Dresser, Co. D, and private David H. Walrath, of Co. F. The regiment in this battle was commanded by Lt. Col. Spofford. At South Mountain, Sept. 14, Sergt. Charles A. Starin of Co. I, and Christian Ropeter of Co. F, were killed.

At Antietam, Sept. 17, the regiment lost 21 killed on the field, viz:—2d Lieut. Louis Dallarmi (acting Captain), privates John Welsh, and Luther Lasher of Co. B; privates Ira Morris, and Porter Strope, of Co. C; Corp. Henry E. Adams, and private C. Emmett Dunning of Co. D; privates Geo. Sipperly and Corp. Patrick Finnigan of Co. F; privates Zachariah B. Fellows and Patrick Currin, of Co.

G; private Godfrey Glesman, George Glesman, and John Levenburgh, of Co. H; Corporals, Wm. Gray, Clinton Ackerman, and Roswell Clark, Jun., Co. I; privates Daniel Horton of Co. I; and privates Storrs, Sherman, Richard Hawley, and John Roberts, of Co. K. Of the wounded, whose number exceeded forty, the following died: private Patrick Connor, Co. G, Sept. 20; Corp. E. Brigham Knight, Co. K, Sept. 21; private Ch'r Moellandick, Co. H, Sept. 29; private Philip Kronmuller, and Nicholas Karl, Co. H, Oct. 7; private James Adsit, Co. F, Oct. Willard Avery, Co. G; and subsequently others whose names are not at hand. From the crossing into Maryland until some weeks after the battle of Antietam, the Regiment was commanded by Major Charles Northup.

LIST OF KILLED AND WOUNDED IN ACTION, IN THE 104th REGT. N. Y. VOLS.

Killed. (At Bull Run, Aug. 30.) 1st Lt. John P Rudd, Corp. Charles Lamont, Co. B; private Lorenzo Compton, Co. B; private John Drew, Co. C; private David Randall, Co. E.

(At Antietam, Sept. 17.) Capt. John Kelly, private Isaac Whitney, Co. C; private Charles V Bush, Co. D; private James O'Hara, Co. D; private John Foster, Co. F; private Verillo H. Robins, Co. F; Corp. Lawrence Sands, Co. D; private Wm. Galvin, Co. D; private Mark Marles, Co. H; private Wm. H. Slocum, Co. H.

Died of wounds received in action. (At Bull Run.) 1st Lieutenant John J. McCaffrey, Sept. 19; private Patrick Baranagan, Co. D, Sept. 12; private

Hugh Johnson, Co. E, Sept. 1; private Herman W Thole, Co. K, Oct. 23.

(At Antietam,) Sergeant Lewis W Shephard, Co. A, Jan. 19, 1863; private Charles N. Crawford, Co. A, Oct. 2; private David M. Catlin, Co. C, Sept. 28; private Harvey Noble, Co. E, Oct. 20; private Elijah Kendall, Co. K, Sept. 24; private John Lyons, Co. K, Sept. 20; private Alexander Massey, Co. K, Sept. 22; private George Garvey, Co. K, Sept. 24.

Wounded in action. (At Bull Run,) 2d Lieutenant Wm. L. Trembly, private George Stryker, Co. A; private Wm. Chizlet, Co. A; private George Hampton Co. A; Corp. Samuel B. Smith, Co. B; private Daniel Smith, Co. B; private Henry Timbrooks, Co. B; private Wm. Jones, Co. B; private Ezekiel Wright, Co. B; private Festus Lafoy, Co. C; private Geo. W Helmer, Co. C; private John Case, Co. C; private Alonzo Austin, Co. D; private Newell W Clark, Co. D; private John D. Towle, Co. D; private Geo. Hartman, Co. D; Corp. Wm. H. Lamson, Co. E; private David Elliott, Co. E; private Chauncey Shriver, Co. E; private Nelson Pennock Co. E; private Francis Roberts, Co. E; private John McCaslin, Co. E; private Levi Van Acker, Co. F; private Wm. McGann, Co. F; private Terrence O'Brien, Co. G; private Thomas Haley, Co. G; private Henry Head, Co. G; private Donald McLeod, Co. G; private Wm. McLeod, Co. G; private John Foley, Co. I; private Michael Higgins, Co. I; private Wm. McGowan, Co. K; private Hiram P Main, Co. K; private Martin Green, Co. K; private Francis Hendrick, Co. K; private Augustus Scotney, Co. K.

(At South Mountain Sept. 14), Color Sergt. Marshall J. Rogers.

(At Antietam), Capt. Henry G. Tuthill; 1st. Lieut. Luman F Dow; 1st. Lieut. Wm. C. Wilson; Corp. Stephen P. Havens, Co. A; private John Westbrook, Co. A; private George Westbrook, Co. A; private Geo. W Mack, Co. A; private Walter Steele, Co. A; private Geo. W Rowell, Co. A; private Wm. Youngs, Co. A; private Wm. Smith, Co. A; private Marcus Hurd, Co. A; private Almond B. Lockwood, Co. B; private Alex. E. Stivers, Co. B; private Lewis R. Campbell, Co. B; private Homer A. Smith, Co. B; private Sidney Miller, Co. B; Sergt. Francis Palmer, Co. C; Sergt. Joseph S. Phillips, Co. C; Corp. Harvey Pike, Co. C; Corp. Francis Twitchell, Co. C; private Oliver Crowell, Co. C; private John D. Myers, Co. C; private Millon Velzey, Co. C; private Allanson J Barnes, Co. C; Corp. Hiram Striver, Co. D; private Philip Fritz, Co. D; private Ephraim Niles, Co D; private Charles Whitford, Co. D; private Jacob Newfang, Co. D; private David Kincade, Co. E; private Charles Gillett, Co. E; private Daniel J. Clark, Co. E; Sergt. John McConnell, Co. F; private John Husson, Co. F; private L. Quackenbush, Co. F; private Stanley G. Merrill, Co. F; private James Drain, Co. E; private Nicholas Hanna, Co. F; private Lorenzo Brainard, Co. G; private Orville A. Perry, Co. G; private Wm. Lee, Co. H; private Cornelius Flavin, Co. H; Sergt. Richard Walker, Co. I; private John A. Baker Co. I; private John Carroll, Co. I; private Thomas

KILLED AND WOUNDED IN THE 107TH PA. VOLS. 153

Higgins, Co. I; private Frederick Sellock, Co. I; private Patrick Mahan, Co. I; private Patrick Walker, Co. I; Corp. Wm. McCracken, Co. K; Corp. Ruel S. Canfield, Co. K; private Francis Seyler, Co. K: private Andrew Reynolds, Co. K; private Dennis Sullivan, Co. K. At Bull Run, the regiment reported 1 officer and 47 men missing.

No list of the casualties of the 105th regiment has been received, and we are therefore unable to include these in this connection.

LIST OF KILLED AND WOUNDED IN ACTION IN THE 107TH PA. VOLS.

Killed, (At Bull Run, Aug. 30) Capt. John T. Dick, private B. F Miller, Co. D; private W H. McBride, Co. F; Corp. S. Lee, Co. G; private George R. Duncan, Co. H; and private John Stondegal, Co. K;

(At South Mountain Sept. 14, 1862) Corp. Wyman Wilcox, Co, G; and Corp. Thos. Dunkinson, Co. K;

(At Antietam Sept. 17,) private Samuel Johnson, Co. A; private Hiram Race, Co. A; private John Miller, Co. B; private Cornelius Ragan, Co. C; private James Gardner, Co. C; private Thomas Kehoe, Co. C; private Thomas Sullivan, Co. D; private Jacob Gorner, Co. E; private Joseph Tomlinson, Co. E; Sergt. Daniel E. Kissel, Co. H; Corp. Martin Lowman, Co. H; Corp. Harrison Mellinger, Co. H; Corp. George W Bryan, Co. H; private George W Foor, Co. H; private Samuel Fesler, Co. H; private John Armstrong, Co. I;

private James Mayhew, Co. K; and private James Mentzer, Co. K.

Died of wounds received in action, (At Antietam) private H. Clay West, Co. A; private David Shugars, Co. B; private Wm. Kendig, Co. B; private W Reaser, Co. C; private James Kauffman, Co. E; private Oliver Cochran, Co. E; private John A. Nale, Co. F; private Joseph Hatch, Co. G;

Wounded in action, (At Rappahannock Station, Aug. 23, 1862) private Adam Benninger, Co. F;

(At Catlett's Station Aug. 24,) private Vintal Miller, Co. G.

(At Thoroughfare Gap, Aug. 28,) private Wm. Swarty, Co. F

(At Bull Run, Aug. 30,) Lieut. John F Williams, privates Lewis Kauffman, George W Readen, and Wm. Shields, Co. B; private Nelson Hawk, Co. C; private Nathan Dinger, Co. D; Sergt. Edward H. Green, Corp. Peter Haden, and John Kauffman, of Co. E; Sergt. Philip Kelly, Co. G; Sergt. George Riley, Co. H; and privates Jesse Adams, and John Darnfeldt, of Co. K.

(At South Mountain, Sept. 14,) private John Dice, Co. B; private Peter Binninger, Co. F; privates John Eidenbaugh, Levi Figart, Jonathan Farr, A. J. Riley, John Pridefelt, Co. H; and private, John Van Dyke, Co. K;

(At Antietam, Sept. 17,) Lieut. George W Z. Black, Sergt. S. A. Hough, Corp. W Seibert, Corp. James Crimmins, and privates George Fake, Ira Hardy, John Hassman, and Cornelius Smith, of Co. A; privates Andrew Ramer, Solomon Slink, and Adam Zain, Co. B; privates James Cronin,

OFFICIAL REPORTS. 155

Thomas Kinsley, Thomas Mullin, and Samuel E. Miller, Co. C; privates John Donahue, and David Bordner, Co. D; Corp. Henry Smyser, and privates James Hosteller, Henry Beener, Horace E. Schepp, and George F Shindler, Co. E; Corp. H. Manweller, privates Moses Carl, and B. Hoyer, Co. G; Sergt. Julius Richter, and James H. Gaster, privates Rufus Byer, and Levi Chaney, Co. H; privates Joseph Gruber, and Jesse Brainard, Co. I; and Corp. Franklin Gordon, Co. K.

Total, killed,   1 officer,   25 men.
    died of wounds,   8
       wounded.   254

OFFICIAL REPORTS.

Head Quarters, 107*th Regt. P. V.;* 1*st Brig.* 2*nd Div.* 1*st Army Corps, Army of the Potomac, Camp near Mercersville Md. Oct.* 8*th* 1862.

To BRIG. GENL. DURYEE, *Commanding Brigade.*

General: For your information I would respectfully present the following report of the operations of the 107th Regt. Pa. Vols. while under my command in the Army of Virginia terminating on the 31st day of August 1862.

Having advanced to the line of the Rapidan August 16th 1862, near to the overwhelming columns of the enemy, the counter movement in the direction of the Rappahannock began on the following day, August 17th, 1862. After undergoing most tedious and fatiguing marches, the north bank of that river at the Rail Road Station was reached on the night of August 19th. On the following day (20th,) the enemy appeared in front from the direction of Culpepper, supposed to be in great force. During this and the next day (the 23d), until 10 o'clock in the forenoon, we were under arms, and in line of battle supporting the batteries in our immediate front and although much exposed during the various Artillery engagements, the casualties were few. Continuing the march towards Warrenton and passing three days near the lines of the enemy in the vicinity of White Sulphur Springs, and village of Waterloo, during which time almost constant artillery skirmishing was going on, your Brigade with the Division (Ricketts's), directed its march on the night of the 27th for Thoroughfare Gap via, Haymarket where it arrived in the afternoon of the 28th and was almost immediately advanced against the enemy said to be Longstreet's Corps, on its way to the support of Jackson, then understood to be engaged with a part of our army near Manassas. Immediately on coming up to your position on the field, your order was given to advance with the 107th to the support of Captain Thompson's Battery on the right of the line, and to protect the line of rail road in that quarter of the field. During the progress of the action this battery was removed to the left of the road leading into the Gap, when your order was received to rejoin the Brigade, then near that point. The action had became during these movements very spirited, and the enemy's skirmishers were being driven into the Gap, and up the mountains on both sides. Meeting you on the road near one of the advanced batteries you ordered me to advance the Regiment to the summit of the ridge on the right. This movement was promptly executed and partly under your own observation and the different numbers of your staff, Capt. Duryée and Lieuts. Neal, Starks and Kenny, through whom I received frequent communications from you during the afternoon. Being on the Ridge we were soon after joined by the 97th, 104th, & 105th, N. Y Regiments which with the 107th, P V compose your brigade, and remained in support of Capt. Matthews Penn. battery until the enemy were driven, as I believe, far into the Gap, when the Division having performed the duty assigned it, darkness approaching and being in danger of large forces of the enemy flanking our small force (being Ricketts's Division only). withdrew via, Haymarket, in the direction of Manassas to Gainseville, where we bivouacked for the night the troops being greatly wearied by the long march and the operations of the day. At the dawn of the next morning (the 29th), we were again upon the road to Manassas where we arrived before noon and unexpectedly found it in the possession of our army After two or three hours rest, the line of march was taken for another battle-field, the battle then raging with great fury near the old Bull Run battle ground. At the close of the day we arrived upon the ground, the battle still in progress, the Rebels being strongly pressed and yielding ground.

The regiment in connection with these composing the Brigade bivouacked on the field while the balls and shells of the enemy were still flying over and around them. Soon after day light next morning (30th), the regiment was in line on the right of the Brigade and moved foward under your orders to the conflict. Forming in line of battle on the extreme right of the front line, and advancing over a ridge obliquely to the left, and relieving the sharp-shooters on our front, and foward to a position in the little valley beyond the ridge, a point considerably nearer to the enemy of any previously occupied by our troops in this part of the field. Being in close proximity to the enemy whose sharp-shooters were endeavoring to pick off officers and men, a number of skirmishers were sent forward to guard against this, and subsequently at your suggestion others were sent forward under direction of 2nd Sergeant J. H. Beamendefer of Co. (I) to ascertain the locality of the enemy's batteries. I would also mention Sergt. Hough of Co. A, as rendering good service in scouting at different times.

The Regiment of this Brigade on our left at this time, began to fire frequent volleys, which soon brought within grape-shot range in a corn field in front a Rebel battery that opened fire with great effect: you yourself receiving a slight wound and contusion from the explosion of a shell. An order was then given to retire some distance, as to have maintained this forward position with no battery of our own available at the time, to reply to that of the enemy, would have been a useless sacrifice of our brave men.

The Regiment on our left in the Brigade retired at once, but not receiving the order I continued to hold the ground occupied by the 107th, and soon after fall back in good order under a heavy fire, and considering the exposed position, with comparativly little loss. A new line was soon formed more in prolongation of the general line of battle in the same woods of the former line, but believed to be better protected from the enemy's batteries. Other movements were made at different times during the day under your orders, which would occupy to much space to give in detail.

On occupying the new position the battle appeared to have slackened by a partial cessation of fire on both sides. Before the Regiment with the others belonging to the Brigade advanced to the position referred to, we received the encouraging word that the enemy was falling back. As we occupied the old ground the firing began to increase, both artillery and musketry, principally to the left of our position, but gradually approaching. It was now evident that instead of falling back and leaving us the victory, as supposed, they had received heavy reinforcements and were in the act of making a most desperate attempt to drive our forces from the field.

For hours the battle grew in volume and intensity. At about 5 o'clock in the afternoon the firing was terrific in the extreme. Gradually the Regiments on the left of your brigade retired and the enemy immediately in front in large force with batteries advanced, with columns of infantry, the Regiments on our immediate left and in our Brigade retired leaving the 107th Regt. (the order to fall back not having been received by me) the only one in position along the whole front of this part of the field. The firing was very heavy and was now, more than at any previous time during the day, being rapidly concentrated against us and in the face of what I think was an effective fire from our side. Being flanked on both sides, our supports all gone and in a very brief period, sure to be surrounded and the Regiment lost, we moved back under a destructive fire in the direction of the supporting regiments and others that had preceded us. As soon as we reached proper ground (having been in a thick wood nearly all the day), we rallied as many of the men as practicable in the growing darkness.

Meeting with you, General, on the same ground rallying the Brigade, and soon after with you at our head we took up the line of march to Centreville, at which point the army was to concentrate for further action, and where we arrived at the dawn of the next morning, being the 31st of August, 1862.

In reviewing the conduct of the Regiment I had the honor to command during the memorable operations of which the foregoing is a very brief account, it affords me great satisfaction to have it in my power to say, that it was uniformly such as was worthy the patriotic and the brave volunteer soldier fighting in defence of his beloved country and its constituted authorities. Although victory did not crown their brave efforts, they bravely performed

REPORT OF COL. MCCOY. 161

every duty and no failure to accomplish any object can be chargeable to them.

The company officers who were present in all or part of the foregoing fifteen days and nights operations in Virginia were Co. A Capt. Jacob Dorsheimer, Lieutenants T. K. Shaffer, O. P Stair; Co. B Capt. J. MacThompson, Lieutenants T H. N McPherson, J. V Gish; Co. C 1st Lieutenant James Corcoran commanding company; Co. D 1st Lieut. A. Wilson Norris commanding company; Co. E Capt. E. D. Roath, Lieuts. James Carman, (commanding Co. C at Bull Run) John T. Williams; Co. F Capt. E. W H. Eisenbeise being sick on the 30th 1st Lieut. Oscar Templeton of same company was in command during that day. Co. G 2nd Lieut. Edwin E. Zeigler commanding; Co. H Capt. John F Dick, 2nd Lieut. G. W Z. Black; Co. I Capt. Henry J Sheafer, Lieuts. Wm. N. Black, and D. S. Mathews, the latter rendering good and faithful service as Acting Adjutant until August 28th, when from severe illness was compelled to cease the performance of duty. Co. K Capt. A. J. Brand, Lieut. Benjamin Rhodes. My thanks are due Sergt. Maj. James B. Thomas for aid rendered in the battle of the 30th during which he was Acting Adjutant.

The field officers present and who rendered me much assistance were Lieut. Col. R. W McAllen, and Major J. Forney, and although laboring under disease that would have justified them in being relieved, they remained with the regiment for duty on the march and in the engagements. The for-

21

mer in making a dangerous reconnoisance in the wood on our right, in the battle of Bull Run, narrowly escaped capture by the rebels. Quartermaster Lyon, although absent with the train, was in the line of duty, and its preservation is evidence that his duties were well performed. I am pleased to be assured that Commissary Sergt. Montgomery performed well his different duties. Surgeon Hutchinson and Asst. Surgeon Wescott, were with the regiment in the discharge of their arduous and responsible duties. Rev. W T. Campbell, Chaplain, was with the Regiment and ever willing and prompt in the discharge of duty. The wounded at Thoroughfare Gap, were placed in ambulances to be conveyed under his care by direction of Dr. Heard, Brigade Surgeon, to hospitals at Alexandria, and falling within the line of rebels near Manassas Junction was detained until Sept. 7th. Chaplains being exempt from capture as prisoners of war he was released and remained with our surgeons within the enemy's lines, in assisting to convey the wounded at Bull Run battle ground to places of comfort and safety.

The losses, although not extremely great, being only 125 in killed, wounded and missing, have been severely felt by the Regiment. The lists of casualties have been forwarded to your Head Quarters.

We have to mourn the loss of a brave and worthy officer in Capt. John T. Dick, of Co. H; who was killed on the field in the Battle of Bull Run August 30th, 1862. First Lieut. A. Wilson Norris Co. D; and 2nd Lieut. John F Williams, Co. E; the latter slightly wounded, both good and esteemed officers, were taken prisoners in the same battle and forwarded by the enemy to Richmond. They are now on parole and awaiting exchange to enable them to rejoin the Regiment. Sergt. E. H. Green Co. E, highly commended for good conduct, was also wounded and taken prisoner. The persons of many brave and efficient non-commissioned officers and men are no longer to be seen in the ranks; they are either dead, wounded or prisoners. It gives me pleasure to record that Sergt. Richard Hough, Co. A; Sergt. J. H. Beamendefer, Co. I; Corp. H. W Smyser, Co. E; Corp. Samuel Lahman, Co. G; Corp. Henry Surriver, Co. B; and private Thomas Wheeler, Co. C; have been named to me as worthy to be mentioned as having shown more than usual zeal and courage, and I am happy to learn that the subsequent battles have increased the list of such worthy and gallant soldiers.

    I am, General,
        Most Respectfully,
            Your Obt. Servt.
        T. F. McCoy, *Col. 107th Regt. P V*

Head Qrs. 1st Brig. 2nd Div. 3d Army Corps,
    Near Sharpsburgh, Md., Sept. 20th, 1862.
Captain JOHN W WILLIAMS, *Asst. Adjt. Genl.:*

Sir, I have the honor to report, for the information of the general commanding the division, that on the 14th inst. we arrived at South Mountain, at 5 o'clock P M. pending the conflict on that day. In accordance with orders we turned off to the right from the Hagerstown pike to a mountain road.

On ascending the mountain we were met by General Meade, who urgently desired me to press forward as the Pennsylvania Reserves were engaged with a superior force. Notwithstanding the men had marched from 4 o'clock A. M. until this time, they gave a shout and gained the crest of the mountain. The 105th Regt. N. Y V immediately opened a galling fire, supported by the 97th and 104th N. Y. V and 107th Pa. Vols. In a short time the enemy gave w y and their broken ranks precipitating themselves upon a whole brigade in column closed in mass, the whole broke and fled.

   I have the honor to be,
    Your Obt. Servt.
     A. DURYÉE, *Brig. Genl.*

 Head Qrs. 1st Brig. 2nd Div. 3d Army Corps,
  Near Sharpsburgh, Md., Sept. 20th, 1862.
Captain JOHN W WILLIAMS, *Asst. Adjt. Genl.:*

 Sir, I have the honor to report for the information of the general commanding the division, that on the morning of the 17th, at early dawn, we took the position assigned us on the field of battle as a reserve in support of General Hartsuff for the engagement of the day. The action opened at daylight, but owing to the early fall of General Hartsuff we quickly gained the right of the Division and immediately became hotly engaged with the enemy. The position of the enemy was in a cornfield slightly oblique with two other lines forming an acute angle with the left of the first line.

 There were two batteries on our right which

opened with terrible effect upon the enemy. Our infantry maintaining their ground poured in a flank fire with great execution.

The conflict continued until there were only about 100 men of the 104th and 105th Regiments N Y V left on the right of Brigade. At this point the cannoniers of one of the batteries were compelled to abandon their guns. The remnants of the two regiments above named rallied behind a large rock, and continued to pour in a deadly fire until reinforcements came up and covered the guns.

The enemy's dead upon the field were almost in as perfect lines as if on the dress parade.

It gives me pleasure to say that the men could not have fought with more determination and gallantry.

I have the honor to be,
Your Obt. Servt.
A. DURYEE, *Brig. Gen.*

Head Quarters, 107*th Regt. P. V*
Camp near Mercersville, Md., Oct. 7*th,* 1862.

Lieut. KENNEY, *A. A. A. Gen*:

Sir, I have the honor to make the following report respecting the 107th Regt. Pa. Vols. in the two actions of Sept. 14th and 17th, at South Mountain and Antietam.

Arriving at the base of South Mountain after a wearisome march of seventeen miles on Sept. the 14th, at about $5\frac{1}{2}$ o'clock P. M., we found the enemy fiercely engaged with the Penn. Reserves. I immediately in compliance with orders from Gen.

Duryée, formed in line of battle near the foot of the hill, and gave orders to move forward with fixed bayonets. Nothing could exceed the promptness of both officers and men in the execution of this order; with the most enthusiastic cheers they dashed forward and soon the enemy were scattered, and in much confusion were flying before us. Several times they rallied, and once in particular having gained an admirable position behind a stone fence they appeared determined to hold on to the last. Here it was they sustained their greatest loss. Col. Gale 12th Alabama fell dead, and the Lieut. Col. 5th South Carolina, wounded and taken prisoner. Their stand at this point delayed not the onward movement of the 107th a moment, but in a little while were over the fence and among them, taking 68 prisoners, killing and wounding quite a number, and causing the remainder to fly precipitately to the top of the mountain. Following them up we drove them across the narrow plain on the summit and part way down the other side. Night ended the pursuit, but fearing a surprise, I directed officers and men to rest in line during the night, prepared for any emergency, and threw 200 yards in advance a volunteer picket of 10 men. About 1 o'clock A. M. one of these pickets brought in a rebel Adjt. Gen. who had the temerity to venture close to our lines. In this engagement we lost three men killed and eighteen wounded. This small loss is accounted for by the fact that the rebels being all the while located higher than we, shot too high. In evidence of the truth of this statement our colors were completely riddled, whilst the Color Bearer was in no wise injured.

The next morning, Monday Sept. 15th, we moved forward, and at night crossed the Antietam near Keedysville, bivouacking on the opposite side. On Tuesday afternoon we again moved forward, and after a few miles march the advance of our Corps engaged the enemy, who, located in a favorable position in the woods, made a stubborn resistance, but finally gave way, falling back however but a short distance.

The coveted ground gained by our force and night coming on, no further advance was made, and both armies lay on their arms ready for the fierce fight of to-morrow, our Brigade having reached a point less than half a mile in rear of the outer pickets.

At early dawn agreeable to your orders, I moved the 107th Regt. by the flank to the field on the right. Here forming in column by Division, we moved forward through a narrow strip of timber, gained the night previous, into a ploughed field on the opposite of which Thompson's Pa. Battery had just gotten into position—advancing half way across the field to within easy supporting distance of the battery, we halted for about the space of five minutes, the enemy's shell and round shot flying about us like hail, killing and wounding some of our poor fellows, but not injuring the *morale* of the Regiment in the least. Shortly we were again advancing, and passing the batteries, and over a clover field, reached the spot so frequently mentioned in reports of this battle, a cornfield. Deploying into line, we entered the field and pushed rapidly through to the other side. Here we found in different positions three full Brigades of the enemy. We opened fire at once upon the enemy immediately in our front, and in fifteen minutes compelled him to fall back.

Receiving reinforcements however, he soon regained his position and an unequal contest of nearly three quarters of an hour resulting in forcing us back through the cornfield. Our Brigade had however done its work. We had held at bay a force of the enemy numerically five times our superior, for considerably more than an hour, and at one time driving him. We were now relieved by reinforcements coming up, and retired to the rear. During the balance of the day we were constantly on the *qui vive*, but were not again called into action save to support batteries.

In the battle of Antietam the 107th Regiment had 190 men engaged, and lost 19 men killed and 45 wounded, a total loss of 85 killed and wounded in both engagements. Too much cannot be said of the dashing bravery of both officers and men at South Mountain, or of their heroic firmness and cool bearing when standing *still* in line of battle at Antietam, they for more than an hour received and returned the fire of a force infinitely superior.

With much respect, I am, Sir,
Your Obedient Servt.
JAMES MACTHOMSON,
Capt. Com'g. 107th Pa. Vols., in the engagements of Sept. 14 and 17, 1862.

COL. MCCOY'S REPORT TO GEN. RUSSELL.

Head Quarters 107*th Regt. P. V.,*
Camp Near Mercersville, Md.,
Oct. 3d, 1862.

Gen. A. L. RUSSELL, *Adjt. Gen. of Penn.:*

General, I have the honor to briefly present for your information and for that of his Excellency, Governor Curtin, an account of the operations of the 107th Regt. Penn. Vols. from the period I assumed the command until it arrived at Centerville, on Sunday the 31st of August, 1862.

I lost no time after receiving the commission of his Excellency, in proceeding to join the Regiment which I found in camp at Cedar Mountain, about seven miles south of Culpepper, Va. I found it organized into the Brigade commanded by General A. Duryée, in the Division commanded by Gen. Ricketts in the 3d Army Corps, commanded by General Irwin McDowell, in the "Army of Virginia," commanded by Maj. Gen. John Pope.

It was late in the night of August 15th, 1862, that I succeeded after great labor, and diligent search, amongst the multitude of camps, that lined the hills and valleys of that region, to find the Regiment. I found it under marching orders, and assumed command in the morning, and at once took up the line of march for the Rapidan.

On the evening of the 17th we encamped on the outer line of our Army and near the Rapidan, beyond which it was known that the enemy were in very strong force. On the next day, after the usual inspection of the Sabbath and the Guard mounting, we rested quietly in camp for a few hours, when exciting intelligence was received at Head Quarters, and soon followed by prompt orders for the march, which was soon taken up northward, and continued far into the night, when the weary soldiers sunk upon the ground in order of battle. This rest, although surrounded by none of the usual comforts, was refreshing and greatly needed, for the following days and nights taxed their energies and strength still more thoroughly. Having attained the north bank of the Rappahannock, a day or two's rest were obtained, with some fresh supplies of provisions.

Whilst at this point (the Rappahannock Station) the enemy appeared on the 20th, as was supposed in force, from the direction of Culpepper. There was some skirmishing; we had batteries on both sides of the river; Gen. Pope took his position on a little eminence in front of our Division, from which by signal flags he formed his lines of battle. The enemy did not advance, and our Army bivouacked in the order of battle, the infantry drawn up in supporting columns, so as to be a sure and convenient support to the batteries. The morning of the 21st found us in the same order, which with but slight changes, was maintained during the day. The cannonading commenced about 10 o'clock A. M. and continued with intervals during the whole day, but it was principally north-west of our position, and with a different corps of our Army. During the 22d most of the cannonading was in about the same quarter, with the addition of some on our left. The enemy however having secured position during the night, opened on the morning of the 23d with all their power directly on our front. This artillery battle continued for three hours, almost unabated, and with considerable effect on both sides, the enemy I think suffering considerably more than ourselves, as they advancing appeared more at a disadvantage, and our Artillery was better served. Lieut. Godbold, of Matthews's Penn. Battery, lost a limb by the explosion of a shell just a little to our right and front. A shell exploded almost in the ranks of Co. F, of my Regiment, and fortunately only mortally wounding one and very slightly one or two others of that company. Many narrow escapes were made during these three hours of artillery battle. The soldiers stood it with a becoming courage. After it I felt a greater degree of confidence in my Regiment.

There being a flood in the Rappahannock, and the temporary bridges having given way and were coming down threatening to carry off the rail road bridge, our troops were under the necessity of evacuating the other side of the river and withdrawing to the north side, which was done in good time and in good order, and with little if any loss on our side.

Soon we again took up the line of march, and in the direction of Warrenton, understood as being in the hands of the enemy. The march was continued all day and up to about eleven o'clock at night, when we were ordered to bivouack in a wood, and prohibited from having any fire. The enemy had evacuated Warrenton, or had been driven out by our advance. We directed our march past the town and towards the White Sulphur Springs, about four miles south west of Warrenton, and encamped about three miles from the latter place. All day yesterday and to day an artillery fight was in progress several miles west or northwest of us, understood to be with the corps of Burnside or Sigel. For two or three days McDowell's Army Corps kept possession of the region round about Warrenton, the White Sulphur Springs, and Waterloo, during which our men were short of rations, but making up the deficiency, so far as could be done, by securing green corn, green apples, &c.

On the 27th we left our camp west of Warrenton, our march being through that place in the direction of Centreville, but when arriving at a certain point we turned off to the westward towards Haymarket, and Thoroughfare Gap, through which a day or two before Jackson had passed with a portion of his Army, and from which he was expecting reënforcements. We arrived it is believed in time to drive this (said to be Longstreet's) force into and through the Gap, or such parts of it as had emerged from the Gap. It was soon apparent that the enemy was in our vicinity, and that there would be fighting. In passing through the village of Haymarket, near two miles east of the Gap, those Regiments having knapsacks were required to leave them at that point. We continued to move forward with great caution. On arriving upon the field I was at once ordered with the 107th to the support of Capt. Thompson's Pa. battery on the right, and also to protect the rail road. At this time the fight had commenced briskly. I continued in the duty first assigned me until it was deemed proper to remove Captain Thompson's battery, or that part of it of which we formed the immediate support, to the left and to another part of the field, where other infantry support was convenient, when I was ordered forward to join the Brigade, from which I had thus been temporarily detached. Coming up to the position occupied by Gen. Duryée, I was ordered by him to march my Regiment to an eminence on our right, and form line of battle along the crest of a hill, which manouvre was promptly executed, the men manifesting a most courageous spirit. Here we remained while the action lasted, in support of Capt. Matthews's Pa. Battery.

Our force at this place and engaged in this action was that of Ricketts's Division only, perhaps about 10,000 men, and I presume it was not deemed safe to remain between Jackson and Longstreet, with a force utterly inadequate to contend with either, and besides it was understood that our orders had been filled and the purpose of the expedition accomplished. In leaving this ground we retraced our steps to Haymarket in the night, and thence to Gainseville, where we bivouacked for the remainder of the night, and at daylight of the 29th continued our march, taking the road directly to Manassas, where we arrived during the day, and unexpectedly found the place in the possession of our troops. Our men being very much wore down by the almost incessant marching, excitement, and irregularity in obtaining rations, were greatly in need of rest As much time for this as possible was given, nearly two hours, and then the line of march was taken for the battle field, the battle then raging with great furry near the old Bull Run battle ground. At the close of the day the Division arrived upon the ground, the battle still going on, and our troops with cheers driving the enemy back. We bivouacked on the field while the balls and shells of the enemy were flying over and around us. Although upon the battle field, and upon the eve of another in which it was known we were to take a part, our men I believe rested well and slept soundly.

Soon after daylight of the 30th the Regiment was in line on the right of the Brigade, which Brigade was on the right of the Division, the Division on the right of the field, the 107th leading during the operations of the day, and being on the extreme right. We moved forward to the conflict early in the morning. The firing of the skirmishers on our right and front had already begun. We were formed in line of battle on the extreme right of the field. We advanced over a ridge obliquely to the left, relieving the skirmishers on our front, and pushed forward to a position in the little valley beyond the ridge, a position considerably nearer the enemy than any previously occupied by any of our troops upon that part of the field.

Being in close proximity to the enemy, whose sharp-shooters were endeavoring to pick off our officers and men, I sent forward to guard against surprise, several small parties of skirmishers. The Regiments of our Brigade (97th, 104th, and 105th,

N. Y. V) on our left soon began to fire frequent volleys, and this attracting the attention of the enemy, he turned the fire of a concealed battery upon us. The range being close it was soon discovered that the fire would be, and indeed was being very effective, some in those Regiments and my own were already wounded, together with Gen. Duryée, commanding the Brigade, his wound however being slight. The General now seeing that the position was an unnecessarily exposed one, gave an order to fall back in order to have the advantage of more favorable ground, as to have attempted to maintain this ground without a battery of our own to reply to that of the enemy's, would have been a useless sacrifice of our brave men. The Regiments on our left hastily fell back, and in consequence of not recieving the order, for some time after I maintained my position; but on receiving it, I marched my regiment back in perfect order and rejoined the Brigade. A new line was soon formed more in prolongation of the general line of battle, and some time after, without pressure from the enemy, it was deemed expedient to retire temporarily a few hundred yards, to give room, as was at the time supposed, for our artillery to operate. Co. A (Dorsheimer's) occupying the forward position as a picket. The battle at this time appeared to have slackened by a partial cessation of fire on both sides. Soon however we were again advanced to our former position, with the encouraging word that the enemy was falling back. As we occupied the former ground the firing began to increase, both artillery and musketry, principally on the left of our line. For hours it increased in extent and volume. At about 5 o'clock in the afternoon, the battle was appaling and terrific in the extreme. Our lines were giving way on the left and centre. Gradually the Regiments on the left of our Brigade fell back, and the enemy immediately in front in large force, with batteries advanced in close proximity, the Regiments on our immediate left and in our own Brigade fell rapidly to the rear, leaving my own regiment the only one in position along the whole front of this part of the field. The firing was very heavy and being concentrated against us. Having by this time been flanked on both wings, our supports all gone, and in less than five minutes would have been surrounded by overwhelming numbers, we moved back in the direction of the Regiments that preceded us, under a most destructive fire of artillery and musketry, and at considerable loss in killed, wounded and prisoners. Rallying the Regiment as speedily as possible, yet under the guns of the advancing enemy, in the growing darkness, and now meeting with the General of the Brigade, yet on the field although wounded, and with him at our head took up the line of march for Centreville, where we arrived at the dawn of the next morning.

In reviewing the operations of the Regiment during the past fifteen days, eventfull as they have been, of which the foregoing is but a brief account, I am the more impressed with its good conduct, and that it deserves well of the country and the great commonwealth from which it came. Leading the Brigade that first opened the great battle early in the morning of August 30th 1862, it has the satisfaction to know that it was the last of the whole Army engaged, to leave the line of that battle at the close of the day—unfortunate as the contest of this day may have been to the Army and country, and deeply as we feel chagrined to have retired before the enemy, yet the Regiment feels confidently assured that none of the misfortunes are, or can be chargeable to it, as up to the last moment, and even long beyond any possibility of retrieving the reverse, did it maintain the forward and honorable position it occupied.

For an account of the losses, as well as the names of the officers who took an honorable part in these movements, I would refer you to my official report to General Duryée commanding the Brigade, which I had the honor to forward you.

The 107th Regiment, it affords me pleasure to record, was under fire in the closing part of the battle (being after dark) at Cedar Mountain, August 9th 1862, and was also in the line of battle, although not engaged, at Chantilly, Sept. 1st, 1862, in the forming of which several were wounded, and should I receive reports of these operations from Lieut. Col. McAllen who was in command, I will take pleasure in forwarding them for the information of his Excellency the Governor.

I herewith enclose you a copy of the report of Capt. J MacThomson, of the gallant conduct of the

Regiment in the battles of South Mountain and Antietam, Md., on the 14th and 17th days of September 1862.

I am, General,
Very Respectfully,
Your Obt. Servt.,
T. F McCoy,
Col. 107th Regt P. V

BIOGRAPHICAL NOTES.

The original plan of this volume contemplated a brief notice of the officers of the Brigade Staff, Commanding Officers of each of the Regiments,— and a sketch of each officer who fell in the service during the period in which Gen. Duryée was in command. From causes beyond control, only a portion of these have been obtained, and are here given, in the order of regiments, preceded by a notice of the chief medical officer of the Brigade.

DR. J. THEODORE HEARD, U. S. V., was born in Boston, Mass., May 28, 1836, began the study of medicine in the autumn of 1856, and after being surgical pupil a year in the Massachusetts General Hospital, graduated in July, 1859. After serving three months in charge of one of the districts of the Boston Dispensary as its physician, he sailed for Dublin, entered the Rotunda Hospital as "Interne," and remained several months, receiving honorable testimonials at the close of the term. He afterward continued his studies in Edinburgh, London and Paris, but his plans for further sojourn abroad were diverted by the present war, and he returned in May 1861, to seek an opportunity for service. He was appointed as Assistant Surgeon of the 13th Massachusetts Vols. July 16, 1861, and remained with the regiment, occasionally acting as Surgeon, until May 1st, 1862, when he was appointed Brigade Surgeon. About May 20th, he was assigned to Gen. Duryée's Brigade. He served in this capacity through Pope's campaign and the battles of Maryland, and was appointed Chief Surgeon of Division Oct. 26, 1862. On the 9th of Nov 1862, he was assigned as Medical Director of the First Army Corps, and held this position until the 1st Corps was merged in the 5th, at the beginning of the Campaign of 1864.

CHARLES WHEELOCK, Colonel of the 97th Regiment, was born in Claremont, N. H., Dec. 14, 1812, and removed in early life to Boonville, N Y., where he became engaged in business as a farmer and dealer in produce. After rendering assistance in raising some of the companies of early volunteers enlisted in his vicinity, he received authorization on the 23d of September, for establishing a branch camp at Boonville, at which place the 97th Regiment was formed. Its organization completed on the 18th of February, 1862.

He conducted the regiment to Washington, and directed its movements until the advance from Warrenton late in July, when sickness prevented him from further service, and he did not return to duty until October. He was the senior Colonel of the Brigade at the time of its reorganization in November, and is still in command of his regiment.

JOHN PEMBROKE SPOFFORD, Lieut. Col. of the 97th Regt., is the son of John D. Spofford, and was born at Brockett's Bridge, N. Y., April 10, 1818. He became Lieut. Col. of the 8th N Y Militia Aug. 18, 1842, and for some years before the war was commercial agent for A. W Harrison of Philadelphia, manufacturer of perfumery and inks. In this business he had travelled extensively, and had acquired a large fund of practical knowledge concerning the country.

He commanded the 97th on the advance into Virginia under Gen. Pope, and on all occasions evinced great intelligence and personal bravery. In the cannonade at Cedar Mountain his conduct was particularly admired, as with a clear and confident tone of voice, he bade his men hold firm and steady, assuring them that the end would be right, and by word and example inspired a cheerful influence upon his command.

He was taken prisoner at Gettysburgh, escaped from Libby Prison in the Spring of 1864, was recaptured, and a few weeks after sent with other Union officers to Charleston, where he was placed under the fire of our batteries. He was exchanged early in August 1864.

RICHARD JONES, Capt. Co. E, 97th Regt, was born in Anglesea, North Wales, and emigrated with his father John Jones to Russia, N. Y., in 1832. He was engaged in business as a wagon-maker at Prospect, Oneida Co., at the beginning of the war, and in the fall of 1861 raised a company composed largely of Welch, of which he became Captain. He served with the regiment until wounded in the arm at Bull Run. He was taken to Washington, where his wound proved fatal on the 6th of September. His remains were taken home to Prospect for burial.

Louis Dallarmi, 2d Lieut. of Co. H, 97th Regt., was born at Aschaffenburg in Bavaria, August 25, 1818. In 1834 he entered the Bavarian service as a private and served eighteen years, during which period he rose to the rank of Lieutenant. At its close he received excellent testimonials of good conduct. For some months he was engaged in the Schleswig Holstein campaign. In July 1855 he was married at Stutgart to Miss Catharine Knoller, and from that city he removed to White Lake, on the northern borders of Oneida Co., N. Y., where he engaged in business till the present war.

He assisted in recruiting a company of Germans which entered the 97th Regiment as Co. H. His superior military attainments would have given him a higher rank, had his acquaintance with the English language justified. He was regarded as the best drilled line officer of the regiment, and on the evening before the battle of Antietam, was placed by Gen. Duryée in temporary command of two or three companies consolidated for this occasion. The Captain of his company was then absent, and the First Lieutenant had just before been suspended from command. While marching into battle at the head of his company, he was instantly killed.

Colonel Howard Carrol, of the 105th N. Y. V., was a native of Dublin, and was by profession an engineer. For about seven years previous to the war, he resided in Albany, and was employed as a civil engineer on the N Y. Central rail road. His attention was particularly directed to the construction of wrought iron bridges, of which that over the Mohawk at Schenectady was built under his direction. He was a gentleman of scientific tastes, and highly cultivated intellect, fond of discussions and researches invoving philosophical principles, and very skillful in his profession. He served for some time as Quartermaster in Meagher's Brigade, and upon the formation of the 105th, by consolidation of parts of two organizations, became its Lieutenant Colonel. Upon the resignation of Col. Fuller he succeded to the command, and led the regiment in all its battles, until wounded in the leg at Antietam. He was sent in an ambulance to the Hospital in the Capitol at Washington, where he died, September 29th, aged 35 years. He left a wife and little son who reside in New York city. A monument to his memory has been placed in the Albany Rural Cemetery.

THOMAS A. ZIBGLE, first Colonel of 167th Penn a Regt., was born in York, Pa., Sept. 8, 1824, was educated at Penn'a college Gettysburgh, and joined Company C. of the First Penn. Vols. as a private, in the Mexican War. This regiment participated in the siege of Vera Cruz, and fought at Cerro Gordo, Pasa La Hoya, and Huamantila, and was at the siege of Peubla, and Atlisco. It was left at Puebla, but soon after joined Gen. Scott in the city of Mexico. Ziegle was made first Sergeant and returned as Captain of his company in 1849. He engaged in the study of law, and devoted much attention to millitary subjects, in the course of which he organized an amateur company known as the Worth Infantry, which attained great proficiency and reputation for the accuracy of its drill both as light infantry and zouaves. With this splendid company and the York Rifles, he advanced towards Baltimore at the time of the destruction of rail roads and bridges near that city in April 1861, but these proceedings being stopped, he returned and encamped at York. He was soon appointed Colonel of the 16th militia, of which his own favorite company was a part, and was ordered to Chambersburgh. He served three months under Gen. Patterson, when he returned to Harrisburgh, and his men were mustered out of service on the 20th of July.

On the 15th of August 1861, he was authorized by Secretary Cameron to raise a volunteer regiment, but the quota was not obtained until March 1862. He was commissioned March 7th, and the next day was mustered into the service. His regiment was soon after ordered to Washington, and placed in the Brigade formed under Gen. Duryée. Col. Zeigle served with intelligence and credit in this Brigade, until July 15th, when he died after a short illness, from congestion of the brain, near Warrenton, Va. His remains received funeral honors appropriate to his rank, and were embalmed and sent home to his residence in York, Pa., where they were interred with distinguished civic and military ceremonies.

THOMAS F McCOY, Colonel of the 107th Pa. Vols., was born in the Juniata valley, and educated to the profession of law. In early life he evinced a fondness for military affairs, and was connected with one of the best disciplined companies in the interior of the state.

In the Mexican war, he assisted in raising a company, obtained a Lieutenant's commission in the regular army (11th Infantry), and was soon with his company on the Rio Grande, from whence he proceeded to Vera Cruz, and thence into the interior. His first encounter with the enemy was at the National Bridge, June 11, 1847 He joined the Grand Army under Gen. Scott at Puebla, early in July following, and accompanied the general advance against the city of Mexico, participating in the battles of Contreras, Cherubusco, Molino del Rey, Chapultepec, and Gauto San Cosme. In the bloody battle of Molino del Rey, he was at the close of the fight the ranking officer of his regiment for duty, four superiors having been killed or disabled, and brought off the thinned ranks from the field.

He was brevetted Captain, for distinguished and meritorious conduct at Cherubusco, and remained in command of his company till the close of the war. Returning to private life with an honorable record, he remained until the breaking out of the rebellion, when he was appointed in April 1861, Deputy Quartermaster General of Pennsylvania, and in this position labored day and night in conjunction with the lamented Gen. K. C. Hale, chief of the department, in clothing and fitting out the volunteers of that state for the field.

While holding this office, the death of Col. Zeigle made a vacancy in the 107th, which the line officers of that regiment unanimously invited him to fill,

BIOGRAPHICAL NOTES. 185

and which office he promptly accepted. He joined the regiment on its march to Cedar Mountain, and has since commanded it, except when acting at times as Brigadier General. Col. McCoy resides at Lewiston, Pa., and is a man of middle age, slight frame, and medium stature.

ROBERT W McALLEN, Lieut. Col. of the 107th Pa. Vols., was identified many years with the Citizen Soldiery. Upon the call for 75,000 men at the beginning of the war, he raised a regiment of 1200 men, but was unable to get them accepted as the quota was full. The men were therefore disbanded. Under a subsequent call he began to raise another regiment, to be known as the 108th, but when half full, his command was consolidated with Col. Ziegle's. Although with delicate health, he possessed an energetic will, and participated in all the battles of the campaign, and during a portion of the time was in command. His home residence is Fannettsburg, Franklin Co., Pa.

JOHN T. DICK, Captain of Company II, 107th Pa. Vols., was a son of Capt. Wm. Dick, who served in the war of 1812-15, and lost two fingers of his right hand at Lundy's Lane. The subject of this notice was born at Mercersburgh, Pa., Nov. 7, 1814. He married Elizabeth B. Wilson of that place, Oct. 2, 1838, and previous to the war, was engaged in mercantile business at Baltimore. Joining the 107th Regt. at its formation, he shared its fortunes until his death, which occurred on the 30th of August, 1862, at the second battle of Bull Run.

THE SECOND BATTLE OF BULL RUN.

"On the evening of the 29th of Aug., Ricketts's Division arrived from Thoroughfare Gap, upon the field, and from an eminence viewed the battle then raging in front.

The whole field was blazing with the fire of artillery and infantry. Cheers ran along the line; and the artillery, with inconceivable rapidity, belched forth the death dealing shot. The intermingling of the roar of artillery with the rattling of musketry, the moaning scream of shell, and the tempest-tossed earth was a scene never to be forgotten. Victory seemed within our grasp. The men were impatient to be led into the deadly conflict to support their companions; but night closed upon the contest, and they laid down, and slept upon their arms. On the next morning, Duryée's Brigade advanced into the woods directly under the enemy's guns.

A brisk fire of artillery opened upon them, with but little effect; the enemy firing too high. The possession of the woods was hotly contested for, by the infantry with various success during the day, driving each other repeatedly across the old rail road excavation. About three o'clock Gen. Duryêe was ordered to withdraw, and pursue the enemy. He sent back word to the General commanding, that the enemy was not retreating. The Brigade maintained its position, but before word could be returned, the booming of artillery was heard from an unexpected part of the field, on our extreme left. The enemy by a change of disposition, had made a detour from the right, and suddenly fell upon our weakened columns with irresistible fury. The Fifth Zouaves were nearly annihilated, in one fire three hundred and sixty fell. The numerical strength of the Union army at this point, had been much weakened by the withdrawal of troops to strengthen the right. The right was the objective point of the enemy in all the series of battles from the Rapidan river.

This sudden change of disposition was a master piece of generalship, and executed with irresistible impetuosity. The enemy approached a line of batteries of twenty four guns, on the left of Duryée's Brigade. Soon the infantry was seen to run by a flank through the woods, and quickly disappear. In a few moments, they debouched from from their hiding place with a slow step, in order of battle, carrying their pieces in the left hand. Our artillery quickly opened with a terrific fire of cannister and grape. The earth jumped alive with the tempest of shot. Their whole line was enveloped in a cloud of dust. While the fire was so intense, they reeled and staggered towards the centre to close up the fearful gaps. Their colors were dashed to the earth, but soldier after soldier, would seize them, and bear them aloft. Still the massive columns advanced with the same slow and impressive step, not a gun fired, or a bayonet charged. The slaughter was terrible. Our gunners worked their guns from four to five times a minute. They approached, nearer and nearer, and with quivering step closed the gaps, until within a few feet of the guns, when a dash was made, and a deadly hand to hand fight ensued for their posession. The enemy by concentrating his heavy columns on our weakened wing, demonstrated that resistance was in vain. We succeeded in rescuing most of our guns, but several remained in the hands of the enemy. This terrific and sanguinary conflict was impelled, on both sides, by the knowledge that they were fighting upon the old battle field of Bull Run. The enemy had a powerful incentive from the prestige of their first victory, and we on the other hand were determined to efface the memory of the former conflict. But Americans were fighting Americans; and there never was harder fighting on either continent than was displayed upon the memorable field of Bull Run."

THE BATTLES IN MARYLAND.

The following extract from a private letter, written by an officer of rank, whose Brigade was in the hottest of the late battles of Bull Run, Sharpsburgh, and Antietam, is of much interest. It comes glowing from the field of danger and honor, under date of Mercersville, Sept. 30th, 1862, and has been kindly furnished for publication in *The Examiner*.

We have just passed through two of the bloodiest conflicts ever recorded in history. After fatiguing and forced marches, we reached Frederick City on the 13th inst at night. Next morning we took up our line of march in pursuit of the enemy, and overtook him at South Mountain, at 5 o'clock P. M. We turned off from the turnpike to the right, and ascended one of the most difficult and rocky of mountains—not excepting Mt. Washington, N H. The men had marched all day long, the roads being exceedingly dusty, and the weather very warm. Notwithstanding this, the men hearing the rattling of musketry and booming of cannon, were animated with new life. They cheered, and climbed the rocks over fallen trees and loose stones, and quickly gained the crest, in support of the Pennsylvania Reserves. Cheer after cheer followed, and was responded to by the Pennsylvania boys. The 105th immediately became hotly engaged with the enemy, supported by the 97th, 104th, and 107th regiments. The enemy soon gave way, and precipitating themselves upon a rebel column closed in mass, the whole broke and fled. The next morning we followed them up, and at night formed in a wood for the general engagement at Sharpsburgh. Our Division opened the fight. My Brigade was to form the reserve; but somehow or other, I suddenly gained the front and right of our Division. At this point, the battle raged with intense fury. My men fought like demons. They drove the enemy. The artillery on our right, which we also were supporting, were firing with two-second fuse—this will show you the close proximity to the enemy. One of the gunners was carrying a shell to a gun, when the enemy's shell struck the tire of the wheel setting fire to the shell he had in his hand; both shells exploded, and tore every strip of clothing from him in ribbons; yet, strange to say, this young man will recover. My loss is 50 per cent. The enemy's killed lay almost in a perfect line, as if on parade. In one place, 160 lay so close together, that you could not discover one missing. I have been exceedingly fortunate, having been only struck three times, and my horse shot under me. My command has suffered terribly. Out of 3,600 men, I have only 800 or 900 left. I lost heavily at Bull Run, where my Brigade opened the conflict, and was the last to leave the field.

EXTRACT FROM A LETTER.

* * * "Where was the General all this time? In all our accounts of battles lost and won, everybody wants to know where the General was and what he did. Various and novel are the inquiries on this point. The idea that seems to prevail in the crowd is, that the General should be where the pictures place him, in the front of his legions, with drawn sabre and prancing horse, plunging over dead and wounded, into the breach.

I have been in many battles, and have seen generals under varied circumstances; some here, some there, some far into the battle, some at a more respectful distance. Many are the generals in this war, whose lives have been sacrificed from too much zeal in pressing unnecessarily into the dangers of the conflict.

But I have not sat down to write a dissertation upon the dashing bravery, or prudent courage of generals, but to give you a very brief account of the singular association I had with our General of Brigade (General Duryée) in and after the battle of Bull Run No. 2, August 30, 1862. He was one of the ardent kind of generals. He wished to be with his troops, and latterly led them into the battle; hence very early in the engagement, and also early in the day, he was wounded, but not sufficiently severe to take him from the field. This battle lasted from "early morn to dusky eve," and indeed this was the second day of it, but the first day for us, our Division being at Thoroughfare Gap the day before. The part of the battle field in which we operated was generally a wooded region of country, and very little of the movements could be seen, except what took place immediately around us. Frequently during the day, the General, with a handkerchief bound around his wounded wrist, visited the lines of his Brigade, to encourage the men and communicate his orders. In the meantime the battle was thickening, the contest was growing hotter and hotter. The thundering of cannon and the rattling of musketry, was terrible in the extreme, and he who passed through the dangers of that day and survived, will have its remembrance so deeply impressed upon his mind as to have a vivid recollection of it to the latest period of life.

In the middle of the afternoon, the General communicated the cheering information that the enemy were retreating, and that our Army was speedily to follow by all the roads! This the General received from some superior, and at the time believed it was true. But alas for the bright hope it inspired, for it soon gave place to sorrow, sadness and defeat —for this information was soon followed by an advance of Longstreet's fresh columns, as we afterwards learned, with an appalling impetuosity, and our worn out and thinned lines gave way before the irresistible onset, and very soon, and as the day was near its close, our army was almost a mass of fugitives from the field; yet there was no panic, as in the former battle on the same field.

It was now growing into darkness. The enemy's advance appeared to have ceased. Only occasional shells were dropping and exploding around. The officers were busy in rallying their men for miles along the south side of that *classic* stream, which gives its name to this day's conflict. This was preparatory to taking up a new position at Centreville, about six miles rearward, to which the disjointed columns of Pope's army were now tending. In consequence of the little day light that was left but partial progress was made in rallying companies and regiments, and less still in forming brigades and divisions.

Officers were here without their commands, and men were here without their officers. Generals, colonels, and staff officers were found here that had not been seen for hours before; they were here I presume to rally their men and march them to the designated point of concentration, and it is probable that not a few pressed on without waiting to look for the fragments of their commands, presuming that they were far forward in the advance column of safety. Our General was not one of these kind. I was happy to find him at the proper place to rally the Brigade. I found the General cheerful, anxious for the safety of his command, and much exhausted from the hard experiences of the day. Yet what a contrast he presented with his entering the contest in the morning! Be it remembered that our Brigade head quarters were marked for a full complement of staff officers, all well mounted, with many mounted orderlies; indeed the dignity of the high position seemed to be well cared for and preserved. Often in ordinary times a few hours work great changes—but those that are wrought by the contingencies of a day's battle, pen or tongue can scarcely describe. The General was now alone and on foot, having apparently lost every thing in the disastrous tide of battle that swept over the plains of Manassas! From anything that appeared at the time, it would seem as if all that fine array of staff and orderlies had been made captives or were slain in the bloody strife! But now was not the time for inquiries, or laments. The battle was lost, but the glorious cause was as good and righteous as ever. We were yet upon the borders of the bloody ground, safety was at once to be secured, for brighter days were in the future.

"God moves in a mysterious way
His wonders to perform."

* * * And how striking and beautiful it has been illustrated in this wonderful war that—

"Behind a frowning Providence,
He hides a smiling face."

But now the curtain of darkness is around us. We still linger while a victorious and a powerful enemy is gathering his folds around. Perils are in every sound! There goes a shell! It passes over and falls away beyond. Here comes a round shot! We know it by its sound. The tree tops fall before it.

It also falls wide of the mark. There a stray minnie whistles by. We care but little for these missiles, but yet we could not but regard them as admonitory. About this juncture a body of the enemy's cavalry were seen preparing to make a charge upon our little column. We were formed under direction of our General to give them as warm a reception as was in our power, and now waited for their approach. They were slow to advance. I passed forward and made a hasty reconnoissance, and soon returned with the comfortable report that the cavalry had disappeared.

The necessity of moving was now urgent. But here a difficulty presented itself. The General was on foot and was almost exhausted. It was utterly impossible for him to march on foot with the column. At this juncture a happy thought entered the mind of a mounted officer present, and who seemed to appreciate the emergency. His mind recurred I suppose to the period of youth in the rural region in which he dwelt, when it was not unfashionable to ride double, and in very extreme cases triple. Two officers were therefore promptly mounted on the same horse, and the General being the senior in rank, was placed in the saddle. Thus formed, the column moved, gathering strength as it advanced. Long, weary, and novel was this movement. It was my first retreat from a battle field. There seemed no end to the column, and not much military precision was observed. Frequently the road was too contracted to allow the doubled up columns and fragments of columns to pass, and being extremely dark, there were occasionally scenes of the greatest confusion. The march continued however, although the men were becoming wearied, as could be observed by the many camp fires that were now flanking the line of march. Duryée's Brigade (the name of the Brigade which was well known and was frequently cried out in the dark to keep the men in the ranks) which had been accumulating in numbers from the start, was now, as we were approaching Cubb Run, being sensibly diminished. It was therefore thought advisable by the General to encamp for a few hours, if not for the night. It was now about midnight, and the men were well nigh exhausted. After crossing Cubb Run the camp fires became still more numerous, and observing a grove of small trees on the left of the road, we filed off into it, stacked arms, and the men after partaking of coffee, the army beverage, rested their weary bodies on mother earth, to sleep, when the recollections of the terrible conflict of the day were, for the time, buried in the depths of oblivion. A very large tree stood near by beneath which the General determined for the time being to establish his head quarters, and groping through the darkness was soon at its base and about to take possession and find a friendly root for a pillow, when he was greeted by a voice of authority, but not offensive, that this was the General's head quarters. General who? was the quick response. Generals Meade and Seymour, was the reply! Well here is a third General, and a Colonel, (introducing himself and his companion) wearied and sleepy, who will if there be no objection join you in your bivouack under the tree. This was cheerfully and politely granted, and the noble tree stood sentinel close over these generals, while nature's sweet restorer was reinvigorating them for the high duties and responsibilities before them. There are strange changes and mutations in men, as well as events in this extraordinary and most eventful period in human affairs. Little did we think or dream, that the gentlemanly officer (then simply a Brigadier,) who welcomed us to this bivouack under the tree, was destined within a year to be the commanding General of the Army of the Potomac, and the hero of Gettysburgh.

A volume might be written of the occurrences of this night. The gory field where we left so many of our dead and wounded, and prisoners. The retreat of our army upon Centreville, into which we entered at daylight in the morning in a heavy rain storm, all of which if put on paper by a skillful pen, would make a work of absorbing interest. The most touching scenes and incidents have been lost in the unfriendly graves that embrace the once living subjects of them: Heaven alone has the record of them.

I need not inform you that at Centreville, in the muddy and crowded streets, the General found his orderlies and horses all safe and sound, they having taken time by the forelock, with visions of Libby, left the field of conflict in time to reach this safe point the night before, and hence were there in time to welcome their General early in the morning."

EXTRACTS FROM THE OFFICIAL REPORT OF GENERAL POPE'S VIRGINIA CAMPAIGN.

(Executive Document, No. 81, Third Session, Thirty-seventh Congress.)

From General Pope's Report, (Page 29).

"Generals Patrick, Doubleday, Hartsuff, Duryée, and Tower, commanded their Brigades in the various operations of this campaign with ability and zeal."

From General McDowell's Report, (Page 52).

"General Ricketts, who, at Cedar Mountain and at Rappahanock Station was under my immediate command and rendered valuable service with the Division, speaks in high terms of the gallantry of Generals Duryée and Tower, both at Thoroughfare Gap and the battle of the 30th, in which the former was slightly, and the latter severely wounded."

From General Rickett's Report, Second Battle of Bull Run, 1862, (Page 70).

"At sunrise on the 30th, ordered by you to send two Brigades to report to General Kearney, and conducted the 1st Brigade, General Duryée 4th Brigade, Colonel Thorburn, which relieved a portion of General Kearney's Division.

"General Duryée's Brigade advanced into the

woods, driving the enemy along the old railroad excavation, until directly under their guns. While occupying this ground General Duryée was subjected to a heavy fire of artillery and infantry, in which he received a slight wound and a severe contusion from a shell, but remained at his post animating his men, who behaved admirably.

* * * In recapitulating the services of brigade commanders I would make particular mention of Brigadier General Duryée for his noble conduct at Thoroughfare Gap, and his indomitable courage displayed at Bull Run, while holding a trying position."

General Meade's report of the Battle of South Mountain speaks highly of the promptness of Gen. Duryée in ascending the mountain in support of the Pennsylvania Reserves, which resulted in the defeat of the enemy.

Battle of Antietam. General Rickett's Report.

"I commend the general good conduct of the Division, and would mention, particularly, Brigadier-General Duryée, Colonels Coulter and Lyle, and Captains Matthews and Thompson of the artillery.

Indeed both officers and men displayed courage under a severe fire."

INDEX.

Ambulance Train narrowly escapes capture, 81.
Antietam, Battle of 115, 158, 190; Duryée's Brigade at, 118; Jackson's account of, 120; Encampment near, 121; Gen. Duryée's Report, 164.
Army Corps reorganized, 122.
Army of Virginia, organized, 39.
Astor Place riots, 11.
Baltimore, Camp of Instruction at, 27.
Banks, Gen., retreats down the Shenandoah, 30.
Banks's Corps, organization of, 39; engaged at Cedar Mountain, 49, 50, 56, 57, 58; guards the trains to Manassas, 85, 103.
Batteries attached to Brigade, 41.
Battles in Maryland, 188.
Berlin, army crosses at, 125.
Bethel, Great, battle of, 21.
Biographical sketch, Gen. Duryée, 9; notes, 178.
Birketsville, hospitals at, 125.
Boonsboro, rebel prisoners at, 114.
Brennan, Sergeant F. J., heroic act of, 97.
Bridge, at Rappahannock, 78, 125; burned by rebels, 112.
Brigade, organized by Gen. Duryée, 29; reorganized, 129.
Brigade Staff, 131.
Bristow, battle of, 84; return of army to, 92.
Bull Pasture mountain, 31.
Bull Run, second battle of, 94, 157, 173, 193.
Burnside, Gen., succeeds to command, 126.
Campbell, Rev. Wm. T., 99, 162.
Carrol, Col. Howard, 43, 181.
Casualties of regiments, 97th N. Y. V., 149: 104th N. Y. V., 150; 107th Pa. V 153.
Catlett's Station, advance to, 30; march from, 33, 42; trains at, 72, 84.

INDEX.

Cavalry, engagement on the Rapidan, 48; rebuked for retreating, 48; raids upon the enemy's lines, 47.
Cedar Mountain, battle of, 49, 50, 169, 177.
Centreville, march to, 38; retreat to, 102, 172.
Chantilly, battle of, 102, 177.
Charleston Mercury's account of rebel movements, 72.
Cloud's Mills, Camp Reliance at, 30.
Consolidation of 105th N. Y. V., 43, 147.
Contrabands' retreat from Culpepper, 72.
Crampton Pass, 113.
Crawford's Brigade advance to Cedar Mountain, 49.
Culpepper, advance to, 47; retreat from, 70.
Dallarmi, Lt. Louis, 181.
Department clerks as nurses, 101.
Dick, Capt. John T., 162, 185.
Duryée, Gen., report South Mountain, 163; report Antietam, 164; obtains leave of absence, 123; resigns, 129.
Dulaney, Col. R. M., rebel, 125.
Fifth Regiment, N. Y. Volunteers, 20.
Flag, designating Division and Brigade, 41.
Frederick City, Maryland, 110.
Front Royal, the enemy surprised, 31; march to, 33, 35; return from, 38.
Fuller, Colonel J. M., 43.
Geary, Gen., at Thoroughfare Gap, 33.
Gibbon, Gen., commands Division, 126.
Godbold, Lt., wounded, 171.
Gordonsville, concentration of the enemy at, 44.
Great Bethel, battle of, 20.
Hall's Battery, 41, 54, 62, 77.
Hall's Hill, retreat to, 103; Harper's Ferry surrendered, 111, 115.
Hart's Ford, encampment at, 43; adventure near, 81.
Hartsuff's Brigade, organization of, 40; reorganized, 129.
Heard, Dr. J. Theodore, 178.
Heintzelman, General, 78, 88, 100, 103.
Hooker, General, 84, 103, 118.
Jackson, "Stonewall," advance upon Front Royal, 31; returns to Richmond, 38; at Cedar Mountain, 51; in the rear of Manassas, 84, 86; at Bull Run, 96; at Frederick City, 110; report of Antietam, 120.
Jones, Capt. Richard, 180.

INDEX.

Killed and wounded, 97th N. Y. V., 149; 104th N. Y. V., 150; 107th Pa. V., 153;
King's Division, 40, 47, 52, 67, 77, 84, 85, 88.
Leppein's Battery, 41, 54, 62.
McAllen, Lt. Col. Robert W., 161, 177, 185.
McClellan, Gen., evacuates Peninsula, 46; in command, 106.
McCoy, Col. T. F., reports, 155, 169; notice of, 42, 123, 183.
McDowell, Gen., march to Manassas, 33, 37; Corps of, organized, 39; report of Cedar Mountain, 60; review of the Virginia campaign, 104.
MacThompson, Capt., 165; reports South Mountain, 177.
Madison Court House, expedition to, 47.
Maine batteries, 41, 54, 62, 77.
Maryland invaded, 106.
Matthew's Battery, 41, 77, 118, 157, 171.
Meade, Gen., 113, 117, 118, 123, 195.
Mercersville, encampment at, 122.
Middleton, wounded at, 111, 112.
Militia called out, 32.
Milroy, Gen., report of Cedar Mountain, 64.
Milroy's Brigade, 31, 52, 81.
Mumford, Col., speech of, 12.
Official reports, 155.
Orders, offensive, 45.
Ord's Division, temporary assignment to, 34.
Pegram's Battery silenced, 56
Peninsula evacuated, 47.
Pennsylvania Reserves, 40, 78, 85, 88, 113, 117, 118, 165.
Plan of attack, Great Bethel, 21.
Pope, Gen., army of Virginia organized, 39; reviews the Brigade, 44; proclamations and orders of, 45; battle of Cedar Mountain, 52, 58; relieved from command, 106.
Porter's Corps, 94, 95, 103.
Promotion of Col. Duryée, 27.
Rappahannock Station, battle of, 75; return to, 70, 127, 156, 170; village burned, 78.
Rapidan, advance to, 66, 169.
Regimental officers commanding, 42, 43.
Regiments, history of organization, 97th N. Y., 145; 104th N. Y., 145; 105th N. Y., 145; 107th Pa., 148.
Reno, General, 52, 72, 78, 88.
Resignation of Col. Duryée, 7th Regt., 15.

Rhode Island Cavalry detached, 30.
Richmond, excursion of 7th Regt. to, 12.
Ricketts's Division, assignment to, 36; organization of, 40.
Ricketts, Gen., relieved, 126.
Riots, Col. Duryée aids to suppress, 11.
Rorbach, Col. J., 42.
Roster, 97th N. Y. vols., 131; 104th N. Y. vols., 135; 105th N. Y. vols., 139; 107th Pa. vols., 142.
Seventh Regiment Militia, 10; escorts Monroe's remains to Richmond, 12.
Seymour, Gen., 195.
Shedd, Col. J. W., 43.
Sigel's Corps, organization of, 39; march to Culpepper, 52, 60, 65; advance to Robinson's river, 67; at Waterloo Bridge, 79, 80; advance towards Manassas, 85, 87, 88.
Skinner, Lt. Col. L. C., 43,
South Mountain, battle of, 112, 114, 188; Gen. Duryée,s report, 163; Capt. Mac Thompson's report, 165.
Spofford, Lt. Col. J. P., 42, 180.
Stevens, Adjutant, account of Great Bethel, 25.
Straggling, fearful instances of, 86, 107.
Stuart's raid to Chambersburgh, 124.
Sulphur Springs battles, 80, 156, 172.
Taylor, Gen. Nelson, 123.
Telegrams, on movements against Jackson, 34; on Rappahannock defense, 76.
Testimonials to Col. Duryée, 16.
Thompson's Battery, 30, 49, 56, 62, 77, 91, 98, 99, 118, 156, 167, 172, 173.
Thoroughfare Gap, 104th N. Y. V. sent to, 33; battle of, 89, 156, 172.
Tower, Gen., wounded, 99.
Tower's Brigade, organization of, 41; reorganized, 129.
Virginia again entered, 125
Von Steinwehr, Gen., orders issued by, 46.
Warrenton, encampment at, 42; advance from, 43; return to, 79, 125, 171; from 85.
Warrenton Sulphur Springs, Banks's sick sent to, 44, battle of, 80,
Waterloo Bridge, advance to, 43; affair at, 88.
Wheelock, Col. Charles, 42, 179.
Ziegle, Col. Thomas A., 42, 182, 184.

www.ingramcontent.com/pod-product-compliance
Lightning Source LLC
Chambersburg PA
CBHW021732220426
43662CB00008B/811